Year 3 Pra

Book

What do you look like?

Draw yourself doing your favourite activity.

This book belongs to ______________________________ .

My class is ______________________________ .

Contents

It is time to do some practice!

3 Draw counters in the blank place value grids to represent the numbers shown.

a)

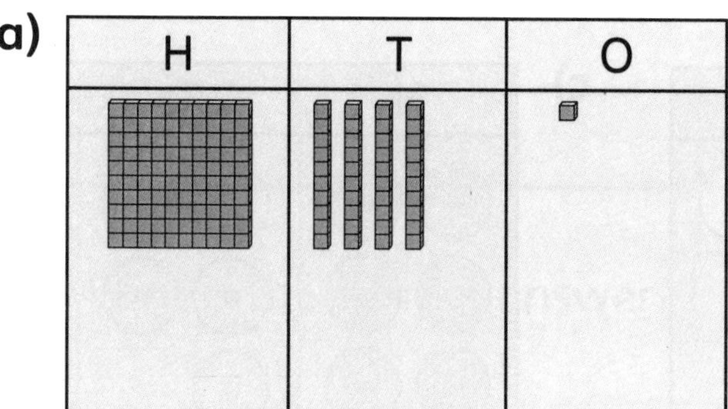

H	T	O

b)

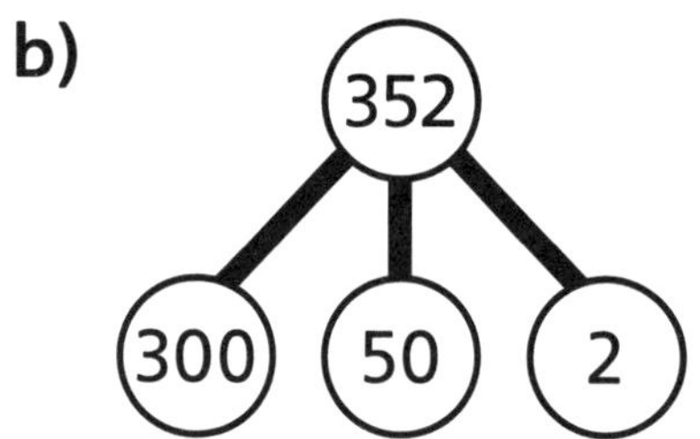

H	T	O

4 Tim has 8 blank counters. 

He places them on a place value grid.

H	T	O

a) What number has Tim made?

Tim has made [ ].

b) He moves a counter from the hundreds to the tens column.

What number has Tim made now?

Tim has now made [ ].

CHALLENGE

5 Helen makes this number.

H	T	O
100 100 100	10	1 1 1 1

Ally makes this number.

H	T	O
100 100	10 10 10 10 10 10 10 10 10 10 10	1 1 1 1

Ally and Helen have made the same number. Explain why.

____

____

Reflect

Make a number in a place value grid using six counters.

How many numbers can you make? How do you know you have them all?

____

____

____

2 Write down three numbers between the two numbers marked.

a) 700 ——— 800 ☐, ☐ and ☐

b) 150 ——— 160 ☐, ☐ and ☐

3 **a)** All these numbers lie between A and B.

What could A and B be?

105	245	176	150	202

A ——— B

A could be ☐. B could be ☐.

b) What is the largest number A could be?

The largest number A could be is ☐.

c) What is the smallest number B could be?

The smallest number B could be is ☐.

CHALLENGE

4 Dafydd marks a number on this number line.

0 100

Decide if each statement is true or false or you cannot tell.

	True	False	Cannot tell
The number is less than 1,000.			
The number is greater than 500.			
The number is less than 700.			
The number ends with a 0.			

Explain to your friend how you know.

Reflect

This number line goes from ☐00 to ☐00.

213 231 312 321

☐00 ☐00

Where does the line start and end? Explain how you know.

→ Textbook 3A p32

Finding 1, 10 and 100 more or less

1 Donna has these apples.

a) How many apples does Donna have?

Donna has ☐ apples.

b) Donna receives another box of 100 apples.

How many apples does she have now?

Donna has ☐ apples now.

2 Work out these amounts.

a) 10 more than

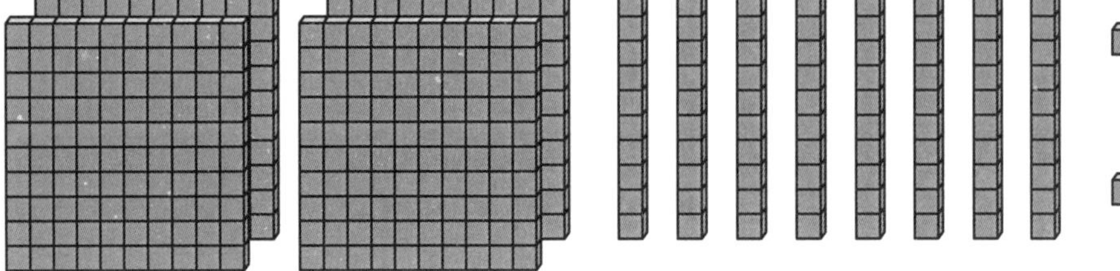

10 more than ☐ is ☐.

b) 100 less than

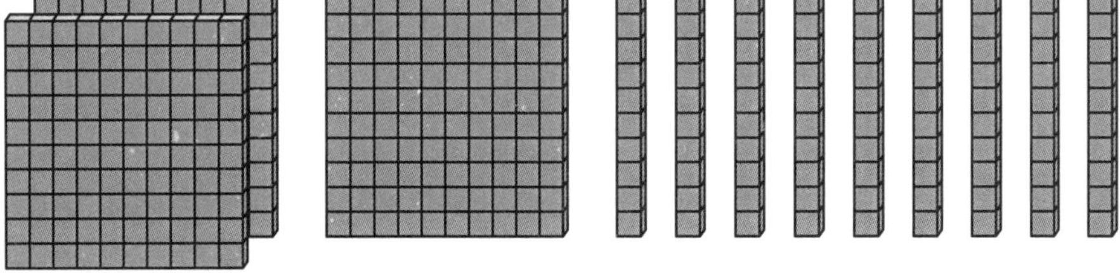

100 less than ☐ is ☐.

3 Complete the sentences.

a) 10 less than

H	T	O
1	2	6

is ☐.

b) 100 more than

H	T	O
7	0	3

is ☐.

c) 10 more than 918 is ☐.

d) 100 more than 755 is ☐.

e) 1 less than 79 is ☐.

f) 100 less than ☐ is 289.

g) 10 less than ☐ is 718.

h) 1 more than ☐ is 115.

4 Mary has the number 700. 

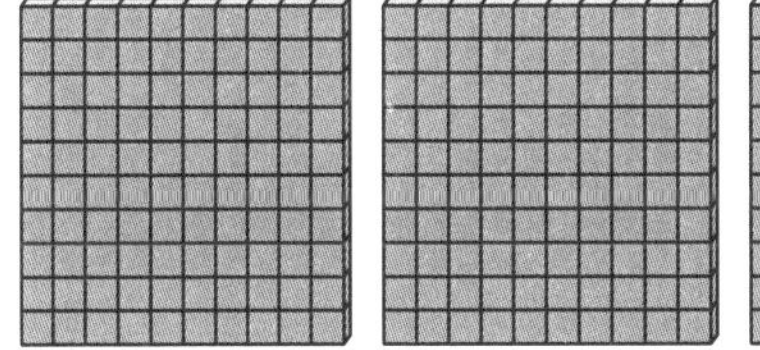 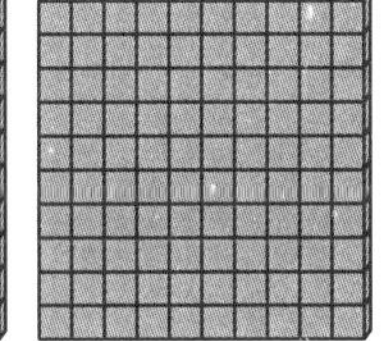 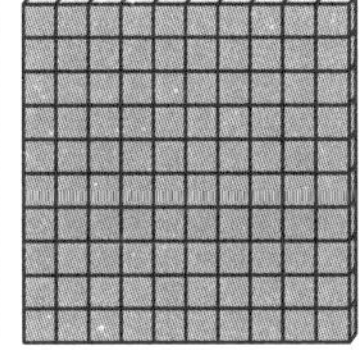  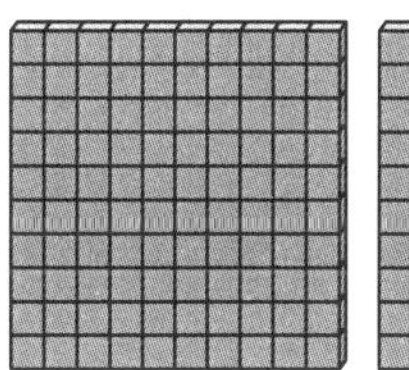 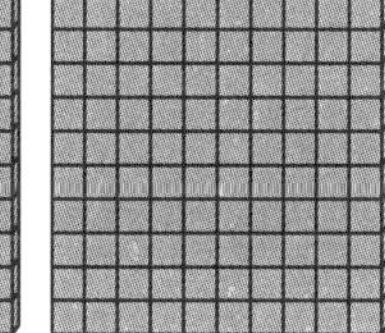

a) Complete the table for Mary's number.

100 more	100 less	10 more	10 less	1 more	1 less

b) Mo did the same for his number. What number did Mo have?

100 more	100 less	10 more	10 less	1 more	1 less
598		508			

Mo had the number ☐.

5 Can you get from Start to Finish on this board?

You can only move one square at a time and go up, down, left or right.

Start 120	10 more	100 more	1 more
10 more	1 less	1 less	10 more
100 more	10 less	10 less	10 less
100 less	100 more	**Finish 309**	100 more

6 **a)** 10 more than my number is 345.

What is 100 more than my number?

b) What is 10 more than 100 less than 238?

Reflect

Roll three dice and make a 3-digit number: ☐

Complete the table for your number.

100 more	**100 less**	**10 more**	**10 less**	**1 more**	**1 less**

Swap with your friend and see if you can work out their number. Explain your working.

→ Textbook 3A p36

Comparing numbers to 1,000 

1 Who has more books?

Mrs Dean

Mr Lopez

Mrs Dean has ☐ books.

Mr Lopez has ☐ books.

☐ is greater than ☐.

So ☐ > ☐

____________________ has more books.

2 Complete the sentences using <, > or =

a) 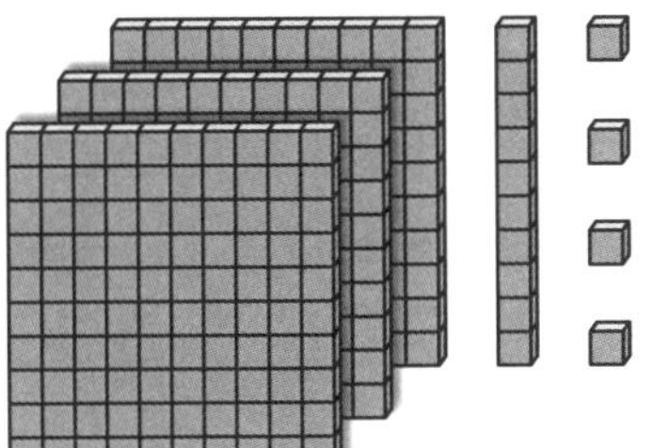  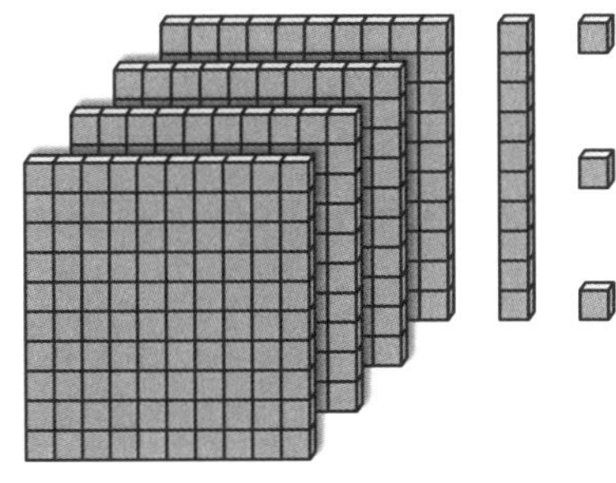

b)

H	T	O

◯

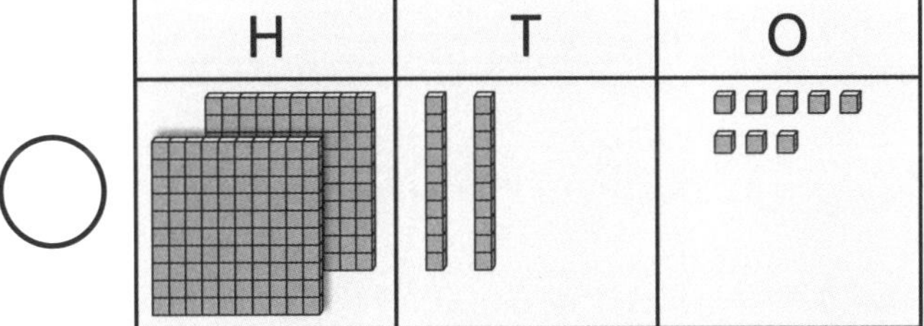

3 Are these statements true or false?

a) is less than 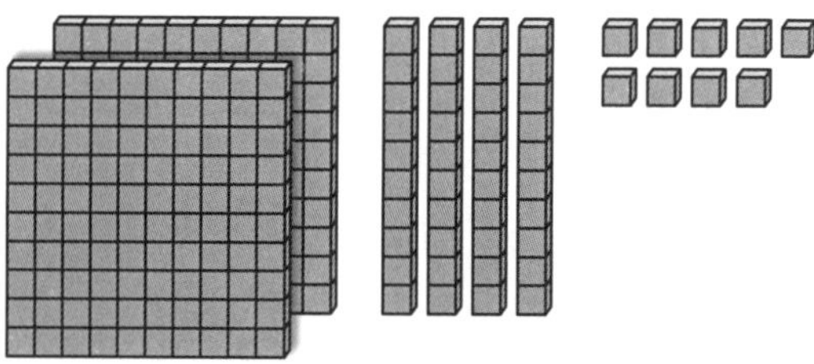

This statement is __________ because ______________________________

____

b) 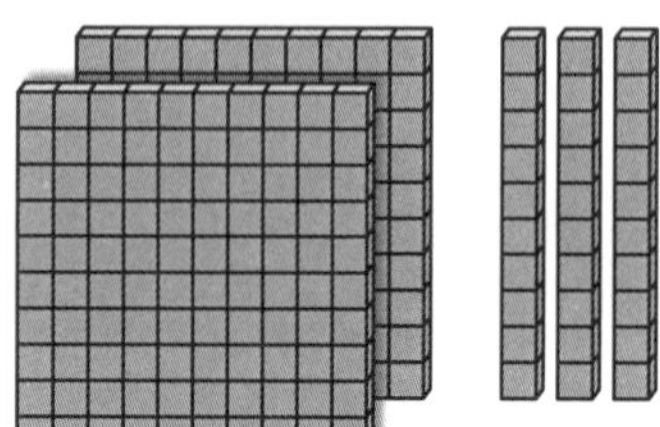 is equal to 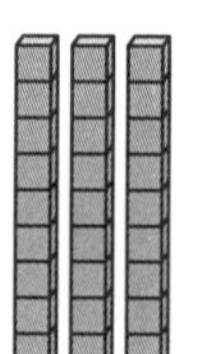 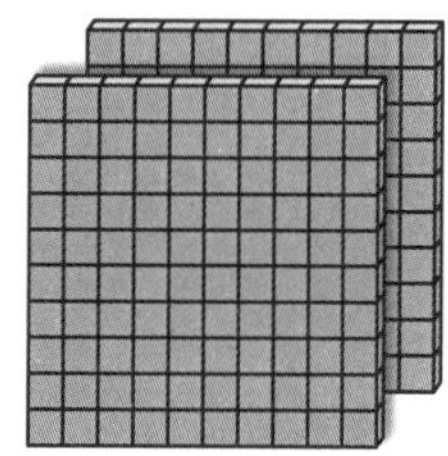

This statement is __________ because ______________________________

____

4 Draw more base 10 equipment to make these statements correct.

a)  <  

b)  = 

5 Which is greater, number A or number B?

A	B
5 hundreds 1 ten 3 ones	5 hundreds 4 tens

_______ is greater than _______ .

You might want to use base 10 equipment to help you.

6 Which number is greater?

Explain your reasoning.

A
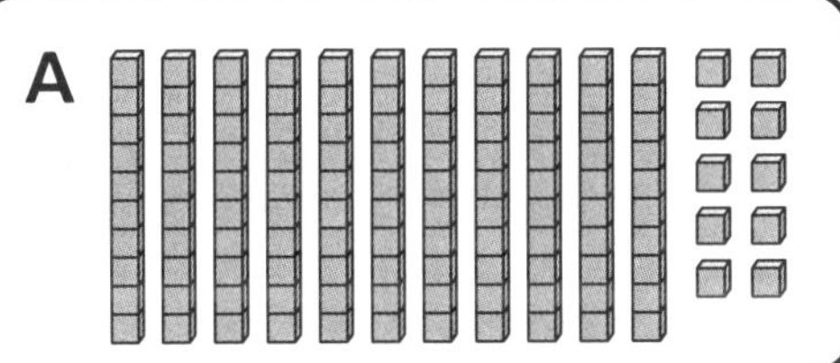

B
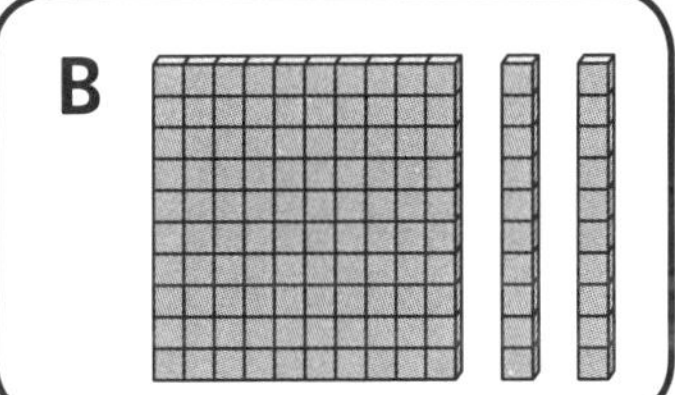

____

____

Reflect

When comparing two 3-digit numbers, what should you compare first?

Explain why.

____

____

→ Textbook 3A p40

Comparing numbers to 1,000 2

a) Which number is greater?

H	T	O
3	4	8

H	T	O
2	5	1

[ ] is greater than [ ].

[ ] is the greater number.

b) Which is the smaller number?

H	T	O
3	6	7

H	T	O
3	8	2

[ ] is less than [ ].

[ ] is the smaller number.

2 a) Circle the numbers that are less than 430.

450   608   900   53   170   340

b) Circle the numbers that are greater than 285.

290   280   286   285   300   29   1,000

3 Complete using <, > or =

a)

H	T	O
1	2	9

◯

H	T	O
2	1	0

b)

H	T	O
9	7	0

◯

H	T	O
0	9	7

c) 309 ◯ 320

d) 494 ◯ 409

e) 718 ◯ 1,000

f) 426 ◯ 400 + 20 + 6

4 Fill in the boxes to make the statements true.

a)

H	T	O
5	6	5

>

H	T	O
5	☐	5

b)

H	T	O
5	6	5

<

H	T	O
5	6	☐

c)

H	T	O
1	4	☐

<

H	T	O
☐	☐	9

d) 38☐ > 3☐7

e) ☐☐6 = ☐3☐

f) 9☐1 < ☐5☐

I wonder how many answers there are for some of these.

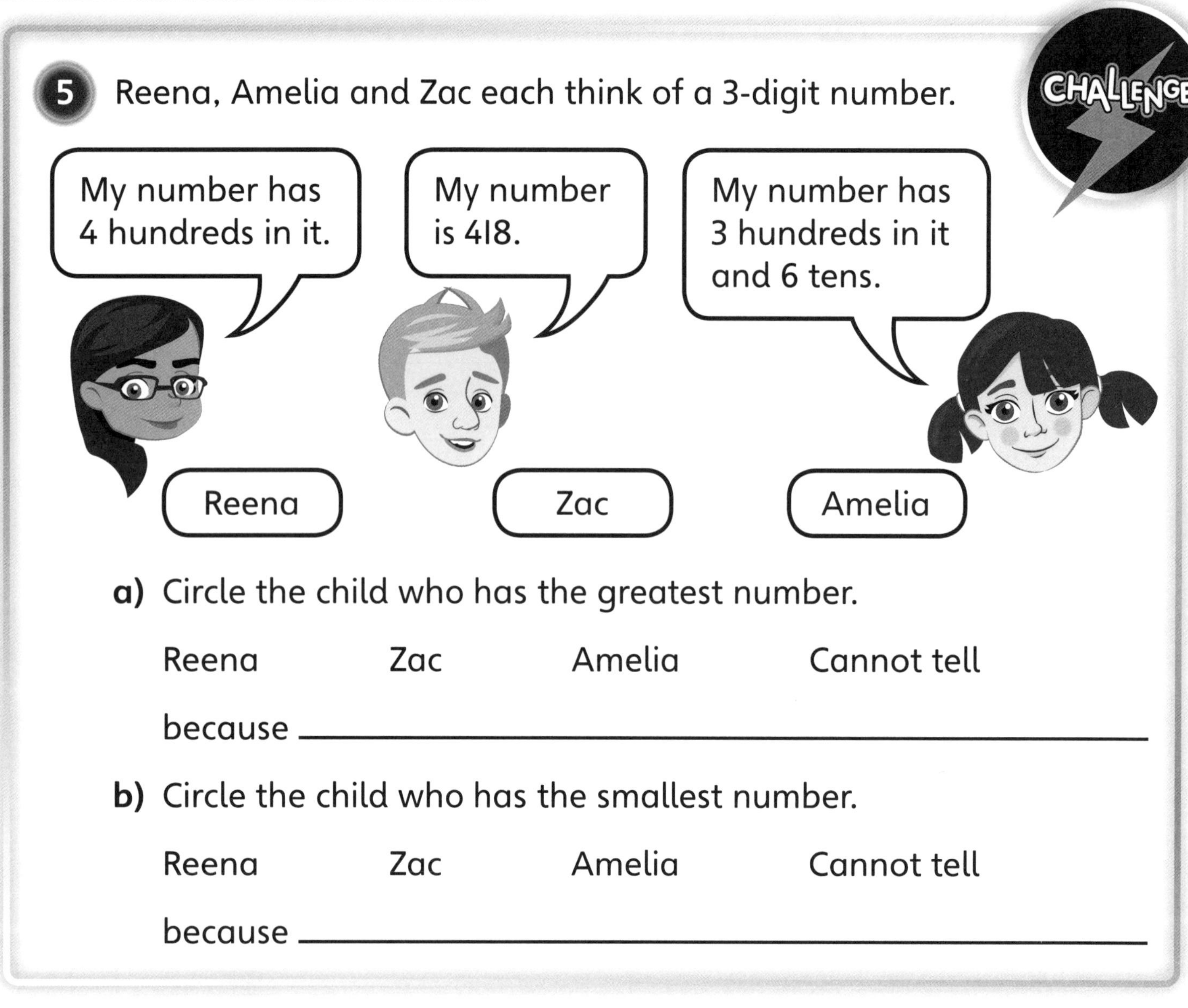

a) Circle the child who has the greatest number.

Reena Zac Amelia Cannot tell

because ______________________________

b) Circle the child who has the smallest number.

Reena Zac Amelia Cannot tell

because ______________________________

Reflect

Work out which number is greater. Explain all the steps.

Use words like first, then, last, 100s, 10s, 1s, compare.

518	514

- ______________________________
- ______________________________
- ______________________________
- ______________________________

→ Textbook 3A p44

Ordering numbers to 1,000

1 Here are three towers and their heights.

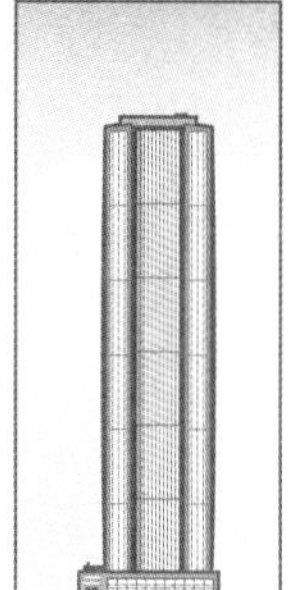

A is 225 metres tall

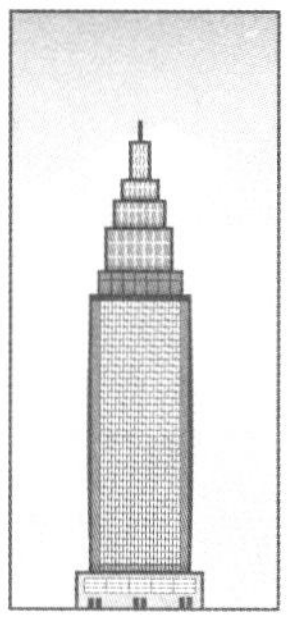

B is 256 metres tall

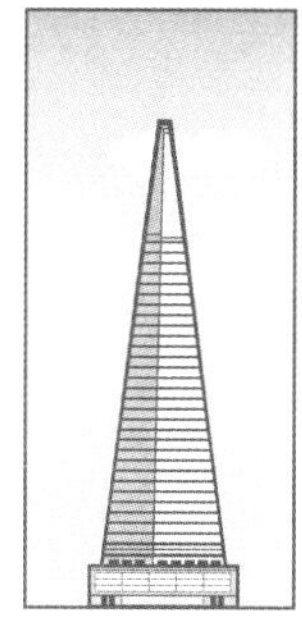

C is 180 metres tall

Put the heights in order.

Start with the shortest.

	H	T	O
Tower A	2	2	5
Tower B	2	5	6
Tower C	1	8	0

__________, __________, __________

shortest tallest

2 Alex has four numbers. He is putting them in order.

417 740 471 74

H	T	O
4	1	7
7	4	0
4	7	1
	7	4

Put the numbers in order, from smallest to greatest.

__________, __________, __________, __________

smallest greatest

3 These are four jars of coins.

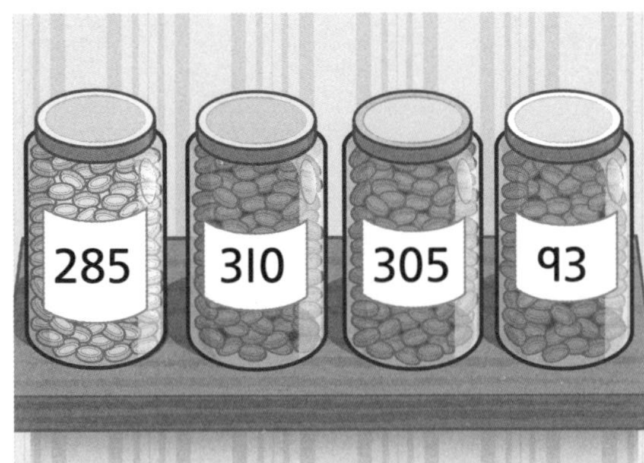

H	T	O

Put the jars in order of numbers of coins.

Start with the jar that has the greatest number of coins.

__________, __________, __________, __________

greatest fewest

4 Order these sets of numbers. Start with the smallest number.

a) 115, 126, 118

b) 295, 200, 529, 207

c) 86, 800, 806, 608

d) 1,000, 780, 70, 80, 870

5 The following numbers are in order.

Find the missing digits.

Find three possible answers for each one.

a) $\square 85 < 39\square < \square 18$ ____________________

$\square 85 < 39\square < \square 18$ ____________________

$\square 85 < 39\square < \square 18$ ____________________

b) $\square 85 > 38\square > \square 18$ ____________________

$\square 85 > 38\square > \square 18$ ____________________

$\square 85 > 38\square > \square 18$ ____________________

Reflect

Look at these numbers and then think about how you would put them in order.

718 817 78 871

____

Explain your method.

- ____________________
- ____________________
-

→ Textbook 3A p48

Counting in 50s

1 Each box contains 50 strawberries.

a) Complete the table.

Number of boxes		Number of strawberries
1		50
2		
3		
4		
8		
10		

b) Circle 550 strawberries.

2 Fill in the missing numbers.

a)

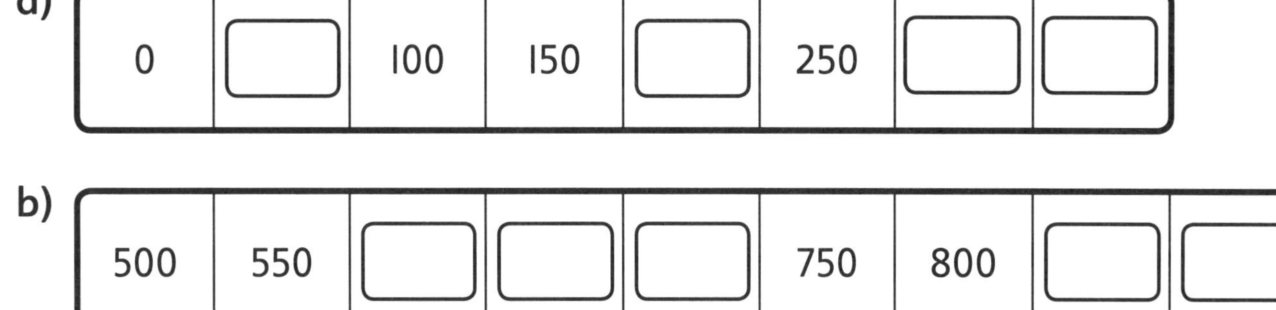

0		100	150		250		

b)

500	550				750	800		

c)

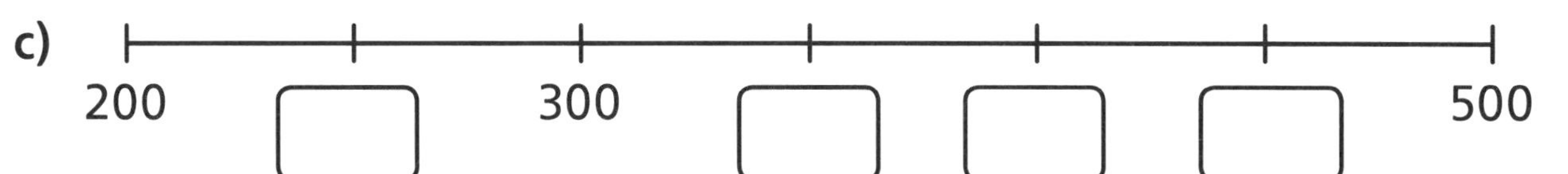

d)

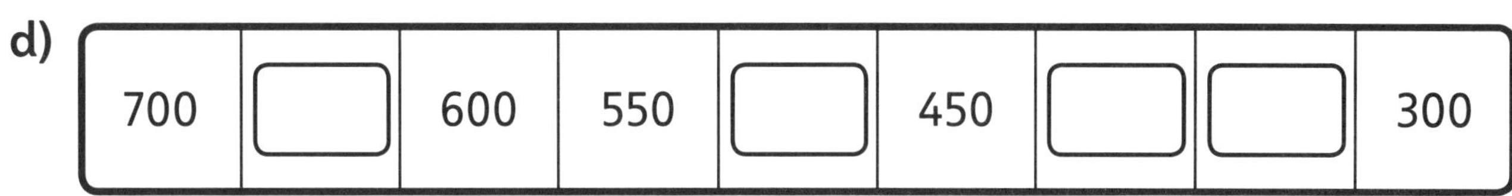

700		600	550		450			300

3 Eko and Allie are playing a game.

The game board goes up in 50s.

Only some of the numbers are shown.

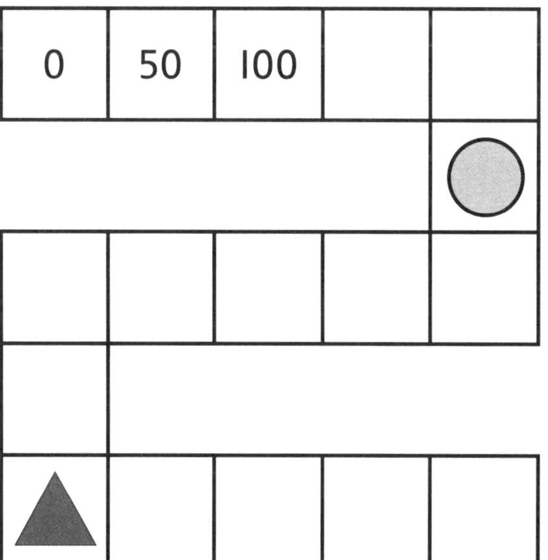

a) Eko is ● and moves forwards 6 squares.

What number does Eko land on?

Eko lands on ☐.

b) Allie is ▲ and moves forward 2 squares.

What number does Allie land on?

Allie lands on ☐.

4 Nails are sold in large boxes of 100 and smaller boxes of 50.

How many nails in total?

a)

There are [ ] nails in total.

b)

There are [ ] nails in total.

5 How many 50p coins in £7?

£1 = 100 pence

CHALLENGE

____

____

____

Reflect

Count in 50s from 0 to 1,000.

Can you see a pattern in the numbers? Explain your answer.

____

____

____

→ Textbook 3A p52

End of unit check

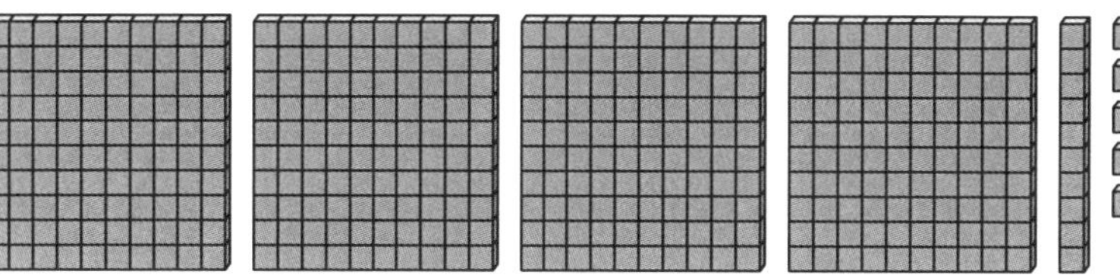

1 What number is shown?

Represent and draw the number in different ways.

Find five ways to describe the number using as many keywords as you can.

Keywords

hundreds, tens, ones, more, less, number line, between

2 Here are seven counters.

H	T	O

How many numbers can you make that are greater than 500 but less than 700?

You must use all the counters.

What happens if you have eight counters?

____

____

____

Power check

How do you feel about your work in this unit?   

Power play

You will need: a place value grid (HTO) and six blank counters.

Place all the counters on the place value grid to make a number.

See if you can find 3-digit numbers to go in the boxes.

H	T	O

	Largest number you can make
	Smallest number you can make
	An odd number greater than 200
	An even number less than 200
	A number that has the same number of 100s and 1s
	A number where 10 more is 241

Put all your numbers on the number line.

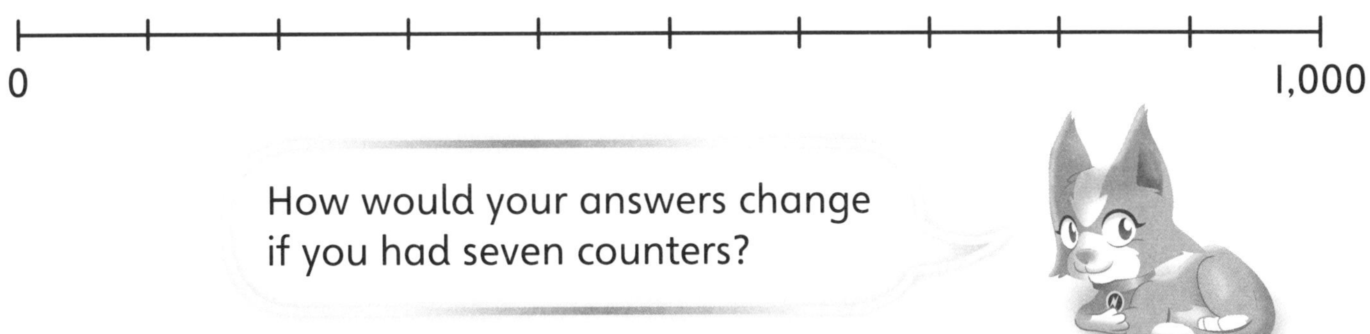

→ Textbook 3A p56

Adding and subtracting 100s

a) George owns a shop. How many ice creams and ice lollies are in the shop?

[ ] hundreds + [ ] hundreds = [ ] hundreds

[ ]00 + [ ]00 = [ ]00

He has [ ] ice creams and lollies altogether.

b) George sells 300 drinks. How many are left?

[ ] hundreds – [ ] hundreds = [ ] hundreds

[ ]00 – [ ]00 = [ ]00 He has [ ] drinks left.

c) How many more ice lollies does George have than choc ices?

[ ]00 ◯ [ ]00 ◯ [ ]00

He has [ ] more ice lollies than choc ices.

d) George gets 200 more of one item. Now he has 600 of that item. What item is it?

____

2 Complete the additions shown.

a) 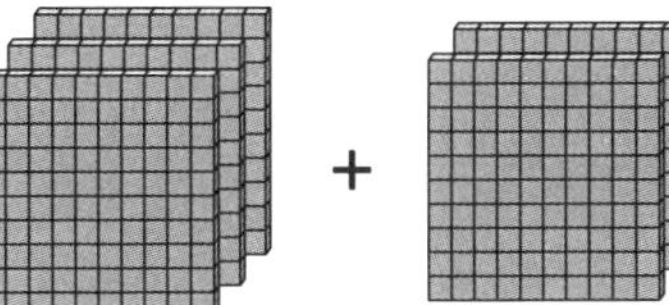 +  = [ ]

[ ]00 + [ ]00 = [ ]00

b)  + [ ] = 

[ ] + [ ] = [ ]

3 Complete the subtractions shown.

a) 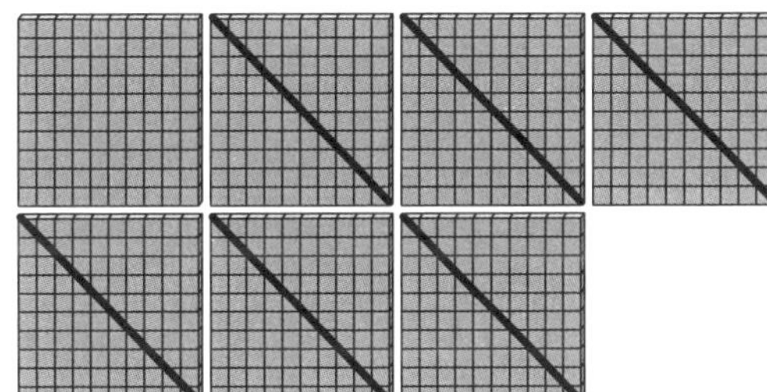

700 – [ ]00 = [ ]00

b)

5	0	0

– [ ] =

2	0	0

5 hundreds – [ ] hundreds = 2 hundreds

4 Circle the calculations that can be solved using this part-whole model. Complete all the subtractions.

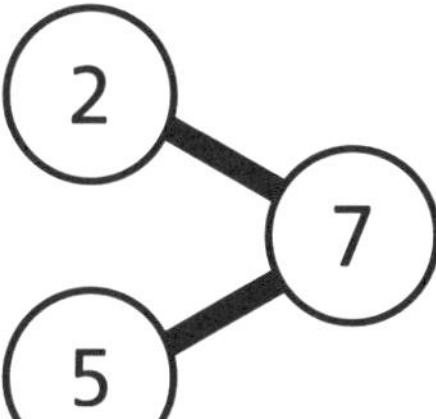

a) 700 – 200 = [ ]

b) 500 – 200 = [ ]

c) 700 – [ ] = 200

d) 700 + 200 = [ ]

e) 500 + [ ] = 700

f) 500 = [ ] – 200

5 Explain the mistake. 

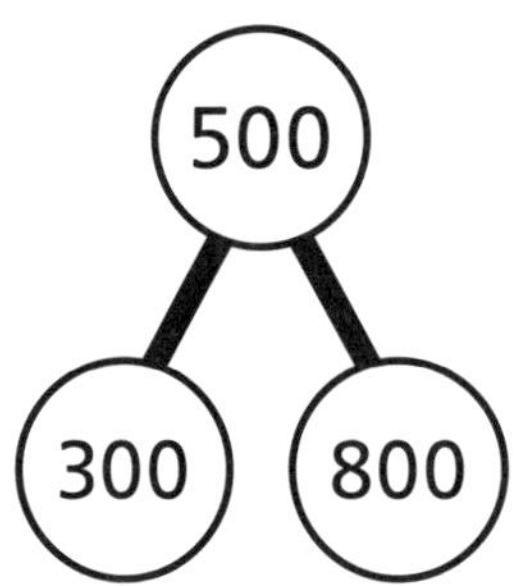

I could try rearranging the numbers.

____

____

____

6 Crack the code. Each symbol represents a single digit. CHALLENGE

△00 – ☆00 = 200

☆ = ☐ △ = ☐

Reflect

How many addition and subtraction facts for 100s can you write that use the number fact 9 – 4 = 5?

- ____
- ____
- ____
-

→ Textbook 3A p60

Adding and subtracting a 3-digit number and 1s

1 A cinema is showing four films.

Film	Angry Fish	Brave Snail	Cool Cucumbers	Dangerous Mouse
	PG	U	U	PG
Number of tickets sold	251	326	140	104

a) 7 more people buy tickets for Angry Fish.

How many tickets is that in total?

1 + 7 = ☐

251 + 7 = ☐

There are ☐ tickets sold for Angry Fish altogether.

H	T	O

b) 4 people leave Brave Snail.

How many people stay?

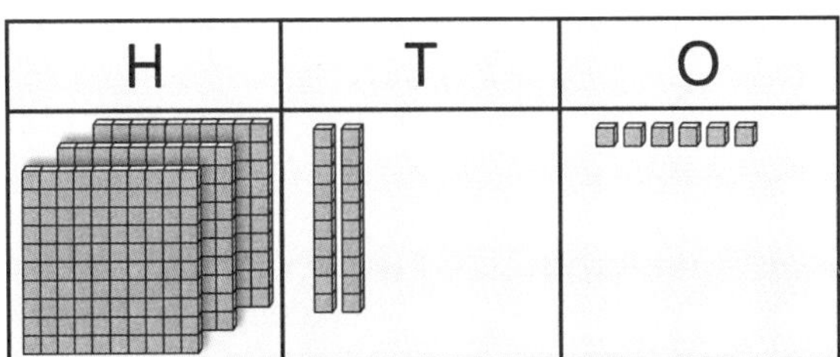

6 – ☐ = ☐

326 – ☐ = ☐

☐ people stay to watch Brave Snail.

2 Complete the sentences.

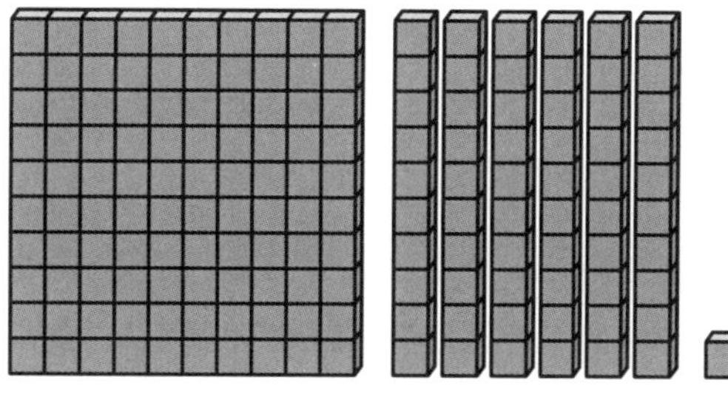

3	5	6

a) Three more than 162 is ☐.

☐ ◯ 3 = ☐

b) Five less than 356 is ☐.

☐ ◯ 5 = ☐

3 Match the calculation to the correct answer. Which one does not have a match?

a) 811 – 3

b) 248 + 7

c) 253 + 5

d) 285 + 3

e) 258 – 3

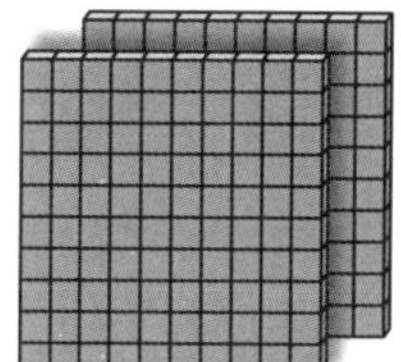

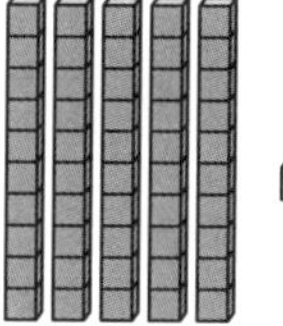

2	5	5

Eight hundred and eight

4 Solve these additions. 

a) ☐ = 315 + 3 **b)** 200 + ☐ = 200 **c)** 514 – ☐ = 511

5 Complete the missing digits and numbers.

a) 5 + 123 = ☐

b) 128 = ☐ + 128

c) ☐23 + 5 = 628

d) 638 = 5 + ☐

6 Use each digit card once to complete all of the number statements.

0	1	2	3	4	5	6	7	8	9

1	5		+		=	1	5	9		
5	4		–		=	5	4	9		
4	3		+		$<$	4	3	4		
	4		–		=	8	4	6	–	

Reflect

Show how to solve 235 – 3 and 235 + 3 using equipment or a drawing.

→ Textbook 3A p64

Adding a 3-digit number and 1s

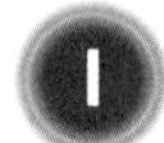

a) A museum has 149 fossils. They are given 5 more.
How many fossils do they have now?

H	T	O

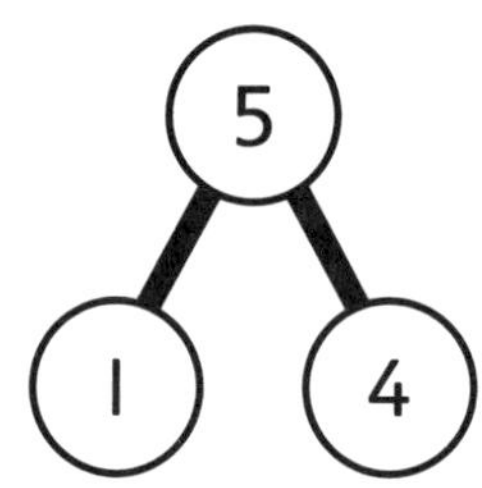

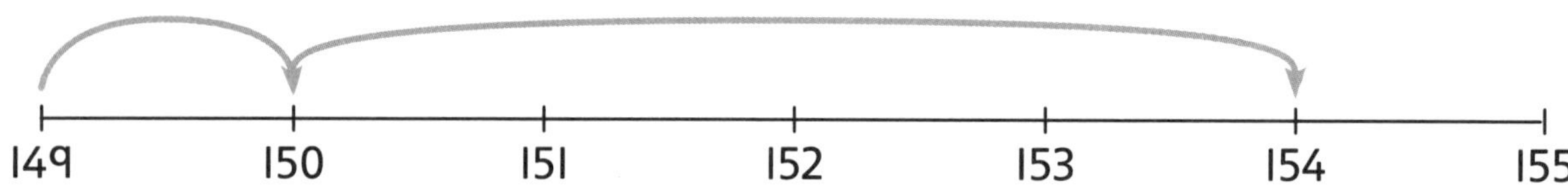

Now they have [ ] fossils.

b) Ella and Noah found 238 dinosaur bones on the beach and 7 more in a field.
How many bones altogether?

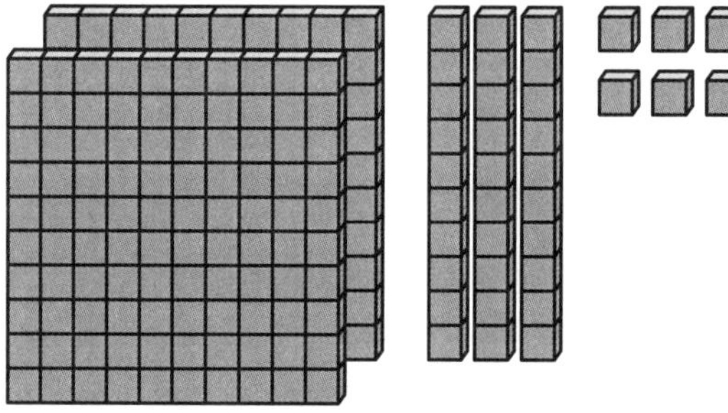

238 + 7 = [ ]

There are [ ] bones altogether.

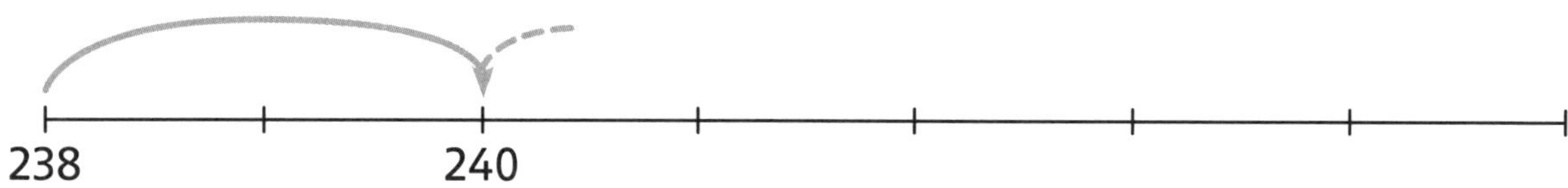

2 Complete the calculations.

3 | 4 | 7 + 4

5 | 2 | 8 + 3

347 350

a) 7 + 4 = ☐

347 + 4 = ☐

b) 8 + 3 = ☐

528 + 3 = ☐

3 Complete the additions.

a) 349 + 6 = ☐

b) 349 + 7 = ☐

c) 349 + 8 = ☐

d) 6 + 459 = ☐

e) 6 + 458 = ☐

f) 6 + 457 = ☐

g) ☐ = 559 + 6

h) ☐ = 558 + 7

i) ☐ = 557 + 8

Explain a pattern that you noticed.

____

____

____

____

4 Circle the calculations where the 10s digit will increase, then calculate the additions.

458 + 1   185 + 4   154 + 8   841 + 5

584 + 1   418 + 5   514 + 8   158 + 4

5 Use the digits 3, 4, 5 and 8 to make additions for each list.

Tens digit will not increase	Tens digit will increase
☐ ☐ ☐ + ☐	☐ ☐ ☐ + ☐
☐ ☐ ☐ + ☐	☐ ☐ ☐ + ☐
☐ ☐ ☐ + ☐	☐ ☐ ☐ + ☐
☐ ☐ ☐ + ☐	☐ ☐ ☐ + ☐
☐ ☐ ☐ + ☐	☐ ☐ ☐ + ☐
☐ ☐ ☐ + ☐	☐ ☐ ☐ + ☐

Reflect

Explain what is the same and what is different about how to solve:
825 + 3 and 825 + 8

→ Textbook 3A p68

Subtracting 1s from a 3-digit number

1 Amy and Bill are selling badges for charity.

a) Amy starts with 251 badges. She sells 7.
How many does she have left?

H	T	O

H	T	O

☐ – ☐ = ☐

Amy has ☐ badges left.

b) Bill starts with 424 badges. He sells 6. How many does he have left?

☐ – ☐ = ☐

Bill has ☐ badges left.

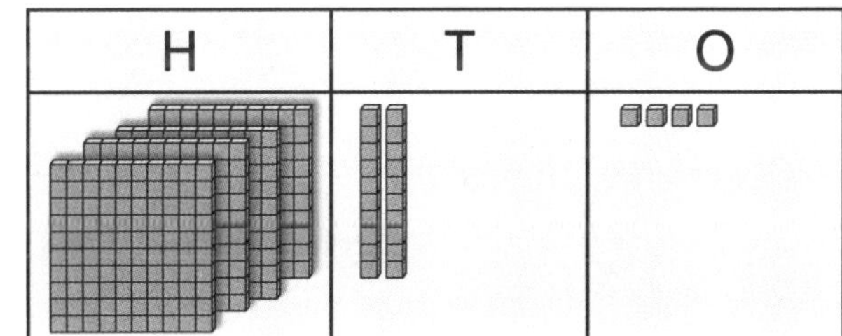

2 Complete the subtractions.

a) 303 – 8 = ☐

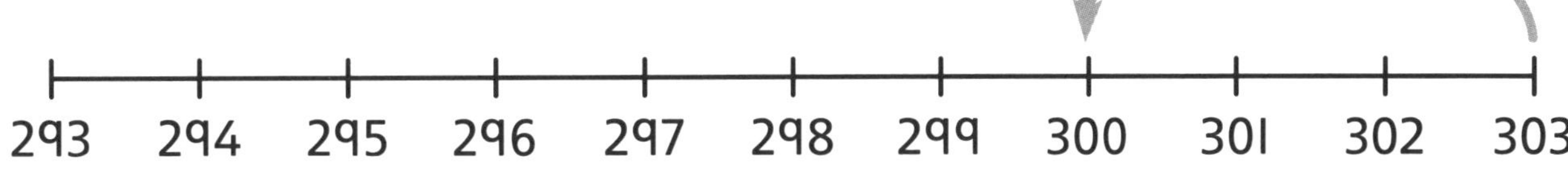

b) 253 – ☐ = 249

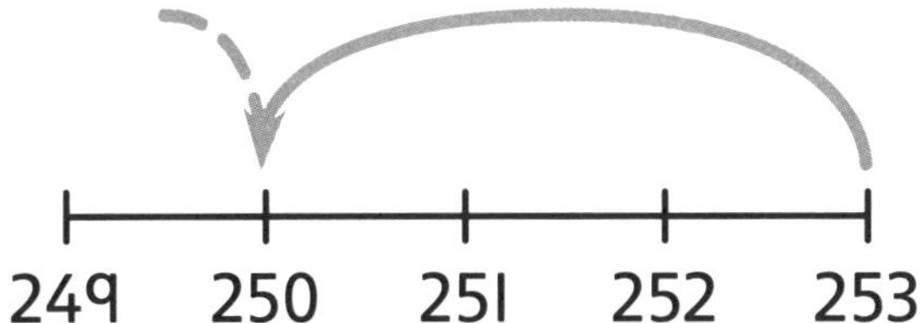

3 Solve each calculation and draw a line to the correct box.

No exchange of 10s		Need to exchange a 10
	135 – 4 = ☐	
	235 – 6 = ☐	
	336 – 9 = ☐	
	446 – 4 = ☐	
	291 – 0 = ☐	
	290 – 1 = ☐	
	299 – 1 = ☐	
	299 – 9 = ☐	

4 Complete these subtractions.

a) 291 – 5 = ☐

b) 391 – 5 = ☐

c) 281 – 5 = ☐

d) 281 – ☐ = 277

e) 314 – 7 = ☐

f) 314 = ☐ – 7

5 Explain Dexter's mistake and describe how to solve the subtraction.

235 – 7 = ?
7 ones – 5 ones = 2 ones
235 – 7 = 232
That can't be right?

CHALLENGE

6 Start on 301. Subtract 9 and find the answer.
Then subtract 9 again. Keep subtracting 9.

301 – 9 = ☐ → ☐ – 9 = ☐ → ☐ – 9 = ☐

Continue the subtractions until you reach below 200.

______

______

______

______

______

______

______

What is the first number you reach that is less than 200?

☐

Reflect

Explain how you know which subtractions need you to exchange a 10.

______

______

______

→ Textbook 3A p72

Adding and subtracting a 3-digit number and 10s

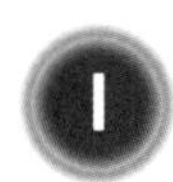

Air team	Fire team	Water team	Earth team
245	157	180	

a) Fire team had 157 points.
They have won 40 more points.

How many points do they have now?

157 + 40 = ☐

They have ☐ points now.

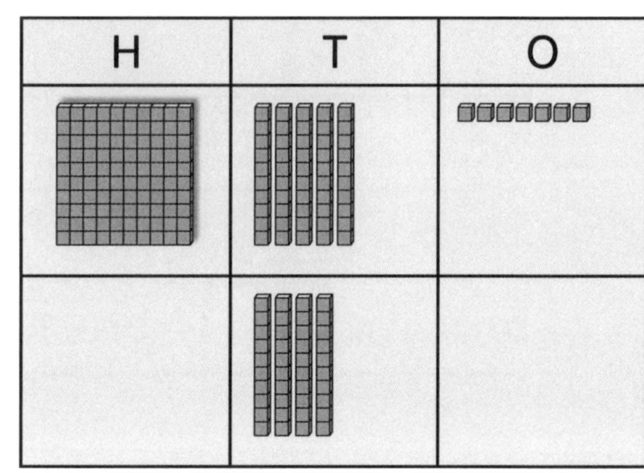

b) Earth team have 50 fewer points than Water team.

☐ – 50 = ☐

Earth team has ☐ points.

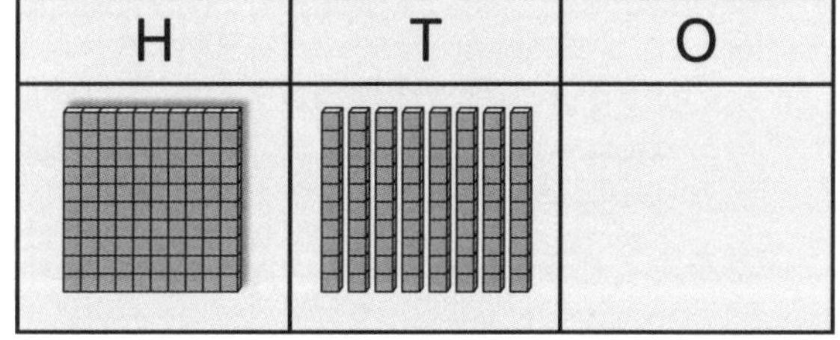

c) A week later, each team is awarded 30 points for singing in assembly. Complete the table to show the new scores.

Air team	Fire team	Water team	Earth team
525	417	310	201

I will add 30 to each score. I will use equipment to check my answers.

2 Complete each sentence.

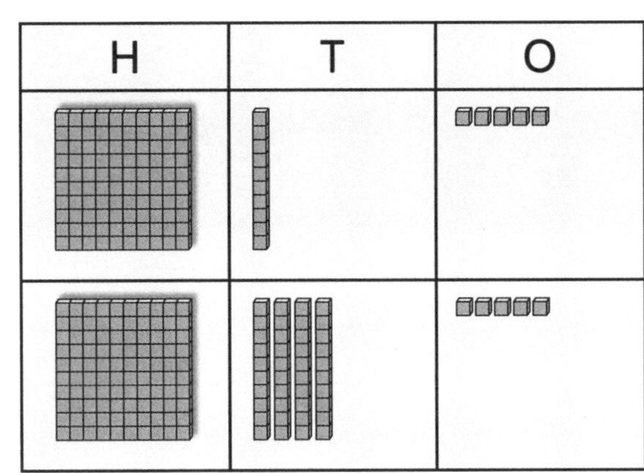

a) 115 is ☐ less than 145.

b) 542 is ☐ more than 522.

c) 537 is ☐ ________ than 527.

d) 883 is 10 less than ☐.

3 Find the missing numbers.

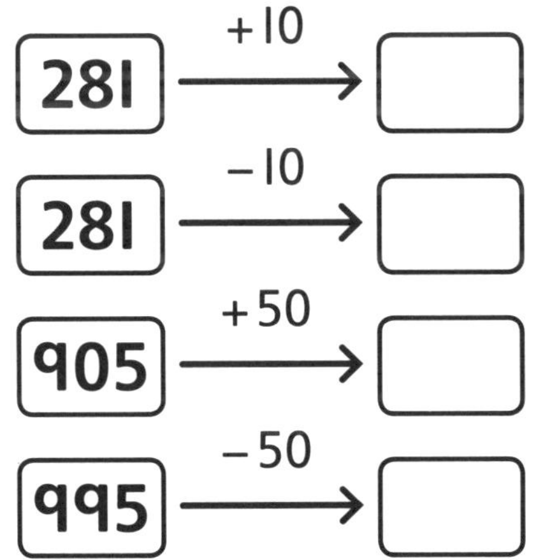

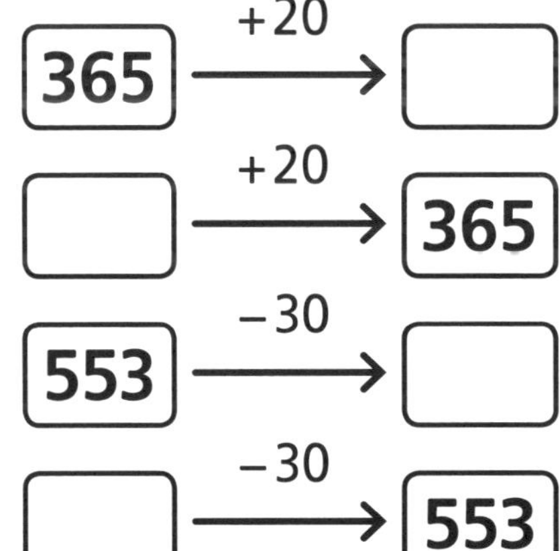

4 Calculate the answer to each calculation and mark it on the number line.

350 – 30 210 + 80 205 + 70 299 – 50

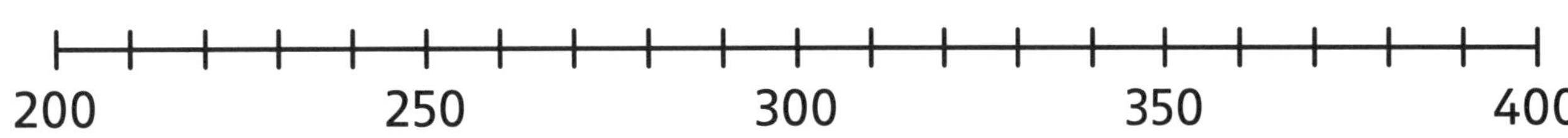

5 Find the solution to each calculation. 

a) 654 + ☐ = 694

b) 654 = ☐ – 30

c) 654 + ☐ = 694 – 20

d) ☐ – 40 = 265 – 20

e) 654 = ☐ + 50

f) 265 + ☐ = 265 – ☐

6 Reuben has 6 extra 10s beads. Write the calculations so that the numbers shown increase by 20 each time from left to right.

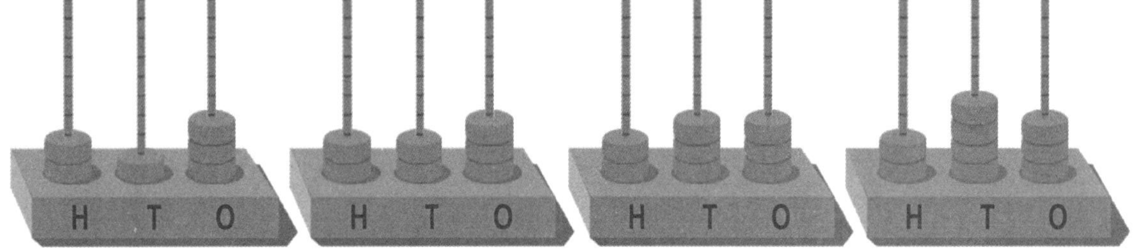

☐ + ☐ = ☐

☐ + ☐ = ☐

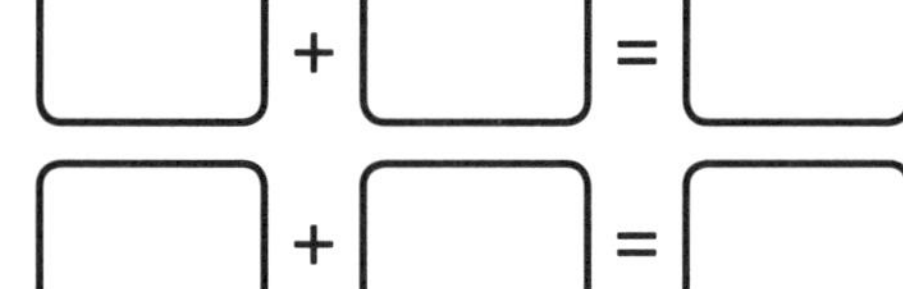

Reflect

What will the 10s digits be in 432 + 60 and in 472 – 40? Explain how you can know without working out the full answer to each calculation.

→ Textbook 3A p76

Adding a 3-digit number and 10s

1 There are 475 people already visiting the castle.

The coach brings 50 more people.

How many people are visiting the castle now?

H	T	O

475 + ☐ = ☐

There are ☐ people visiting the castle now.

2 Richard is using drawings and place value equipment to solve these calculations. Complete his additions.

a) 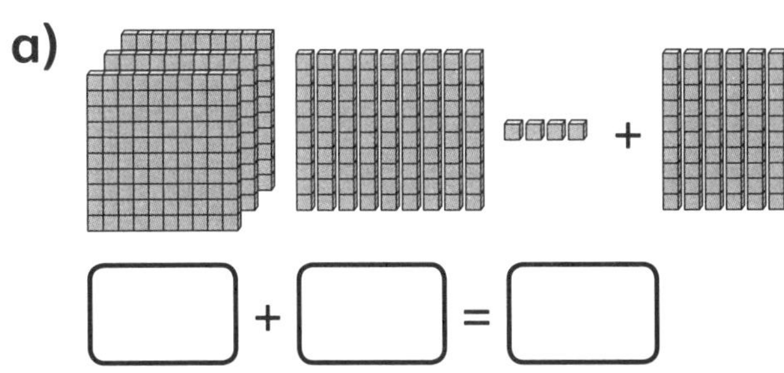

☐ + ☐ = ☐

c) 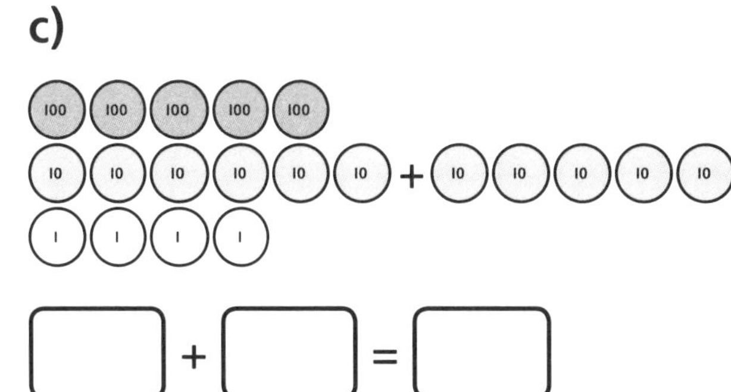

☐ + ☐ = ☐

b) 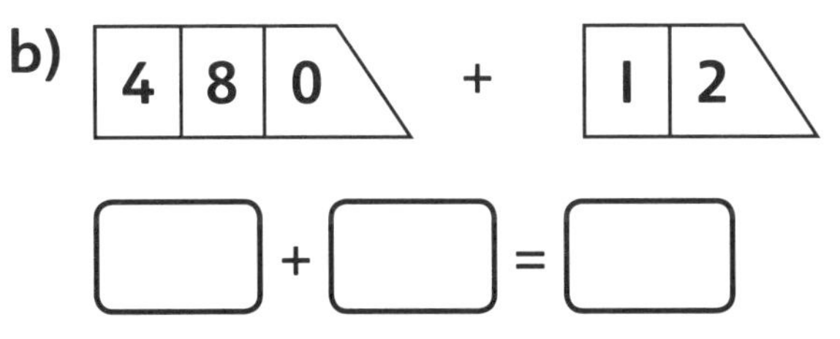

☐ + ☐ = ☐

d) 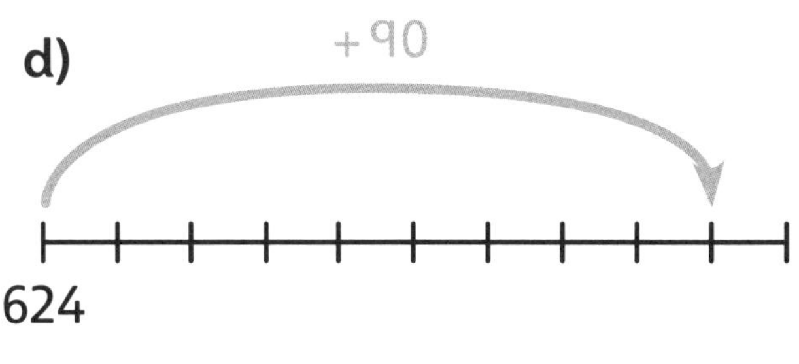

☐ + ☐ = ☐

3 Complete the missing numbers.

a) 234 + 90 = ☐

b) 371 + 50 = ☐ + 60

c) ☐ = 40 + 569

d) 20 + ☐ = 319

e) 50 more than 762 is ☐

f) 150 = ☐ + 90

4 What mistake has Isla made?

____

____

____

____

____

____

5 Solve these additions.

a) 294 + 70 = ☐

b) ☐ = 90 + 326

c) 284 + 80 = ☐

d) ☐ = 70 + 346

e) 274 + 90 = ☐

f) ☐ = 50 + 366

Explain any patterns that you noticed.

____

____

____

CHALLENGE

6 Complete each addition to match each answer shown on the number line.

4 ☐ ☐ + ☐ 0   4 9 ☐ + ☐ 0

500 — 600

☐ 7 ☐ + ☐ 0   4 ☐ ☐ + ☐ 0

I can find more than one addition for some calculations.

Reflect

When I add a 3-digit number and tens, I know I will need to exchange 10 tens for 1 hundred if

→ Textbook 3A p80

Subtracting 10s from a 3-digit number

a) Lucas's book has 225 pages. He has read 70 pages.
How many pages does he have left to read?

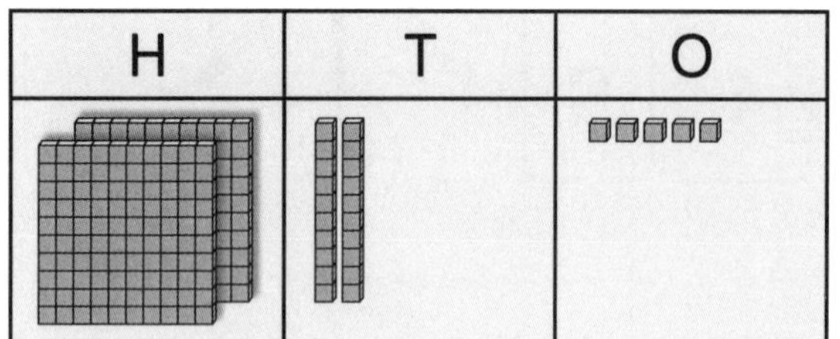

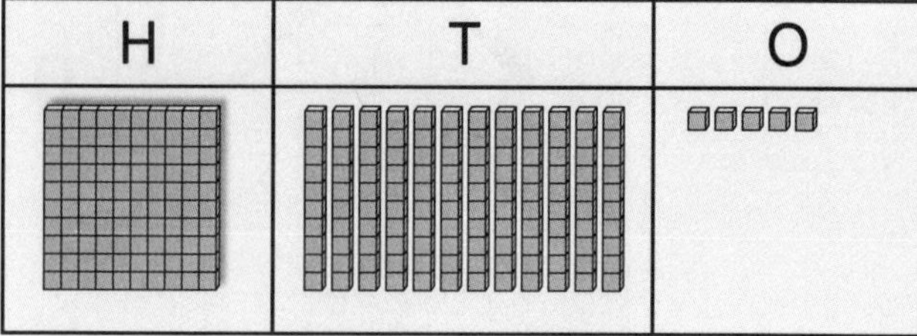

12 tens – [ ] tens = [ ] tens

225 – 70 = [ ]   Lucas has [ ] pages left.

b) Sara's book has 231 pages. She has 60 pages left to read.
How many has she already read?

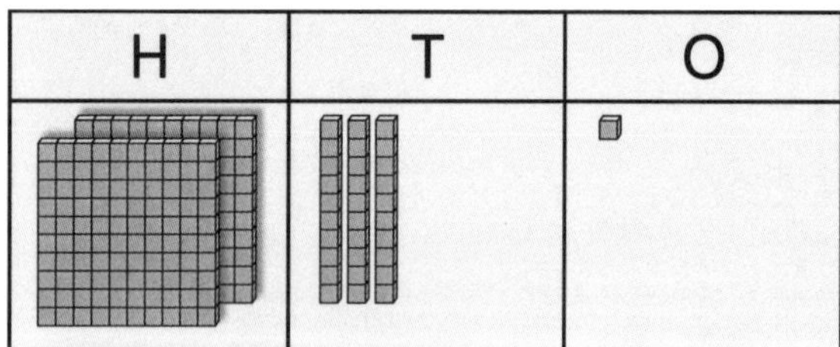

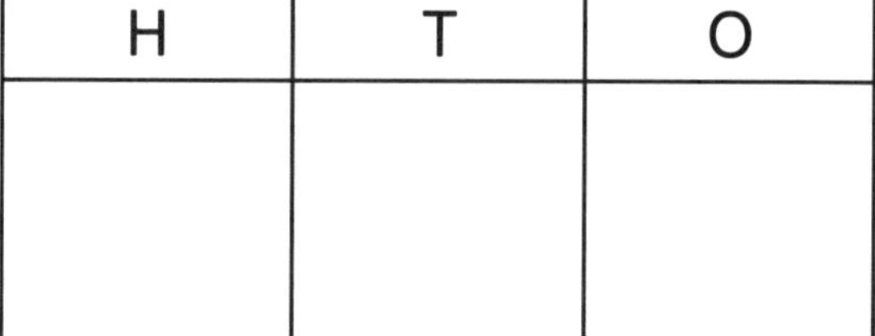

231 – 60 = [ ]   Sara has [ ] pages left.

c) George has read 80 pages. His dad has read 315 pages.
How many more pages has his dad read than George?

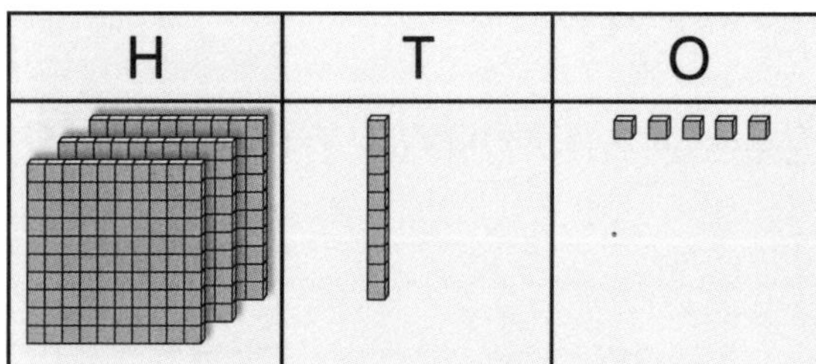

315 ◯ [ ] = [ ]

George's dad has read [ ] more pages.

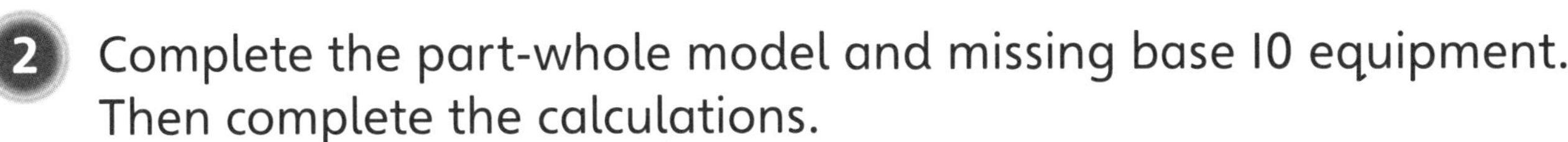

2 Complete the part-whole model and missing base 10 equipment. Then complete the calculations.

a)

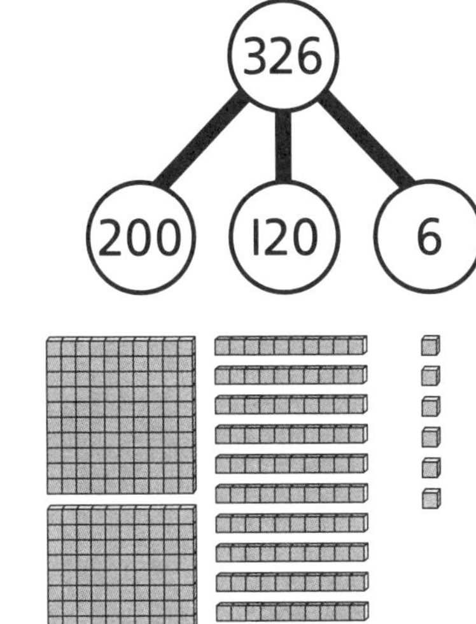

326 – 60 = ☐

b)

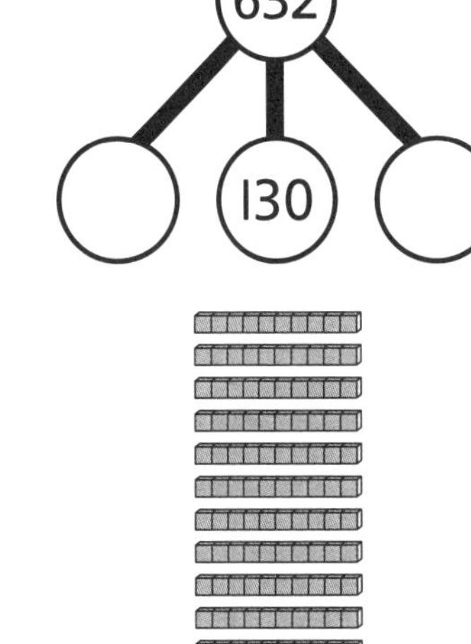

632 – 80 = ☐

3 Find the missing numbers.

30 less	Number	30 more
	215	245
	316	
		300

4 Complete the calculations.

a) 340 – 60 = ☐

b) ☐ = 821 – 70

c) 350 – 60 = ☐

d) ☐ = 831 – 70

5 Complete the calculations to match each answer shown on the number line.

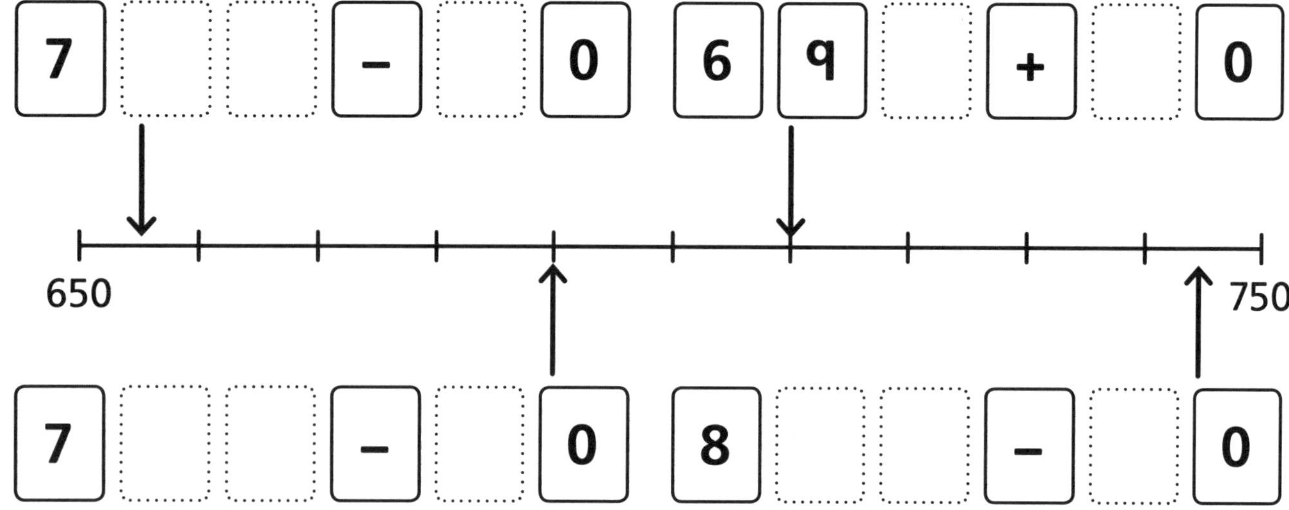

6 Reena thinks of a number. She adds 90, then adds 80, then adds 70. She finishes on a number with the digits 1, 2 and 3. What numbers could she have started on?

Reflect

I know 15 – 8 so I can work out 251 – 80 by

→ Textbook 3A p84

Adding and subtracting a 3-digit and a 2-digit number

a) On Monday a postman delivered 152 letters. On Tuesday he delivered 37 letters. How many letters did he deliver in total?

H	T	O

	H	T	O
	1	5	2
+			

152 + 37 = ☐

He delivered ☐ letters in total.

b) On Friday, the postman delivered 41 fewer letters than on Monday. How many letters did the postman deliver on Friday?

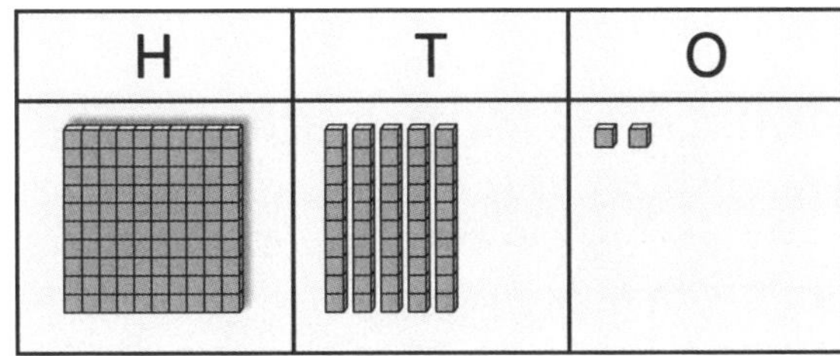

	H	T	O
–			

152 – ☐ = ☐

He delivered ☐ letters on Friday.

2 Match the calculations to the pictures.
Which one does not have a matching picture?

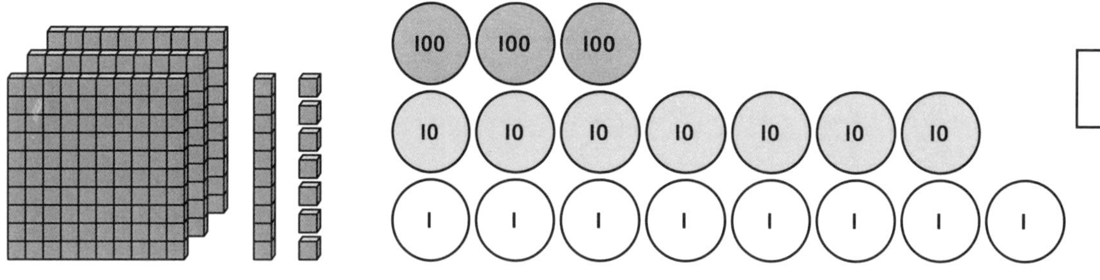

1	6	3

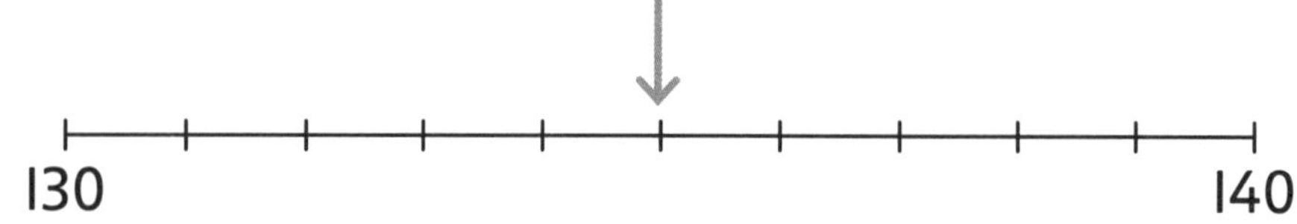

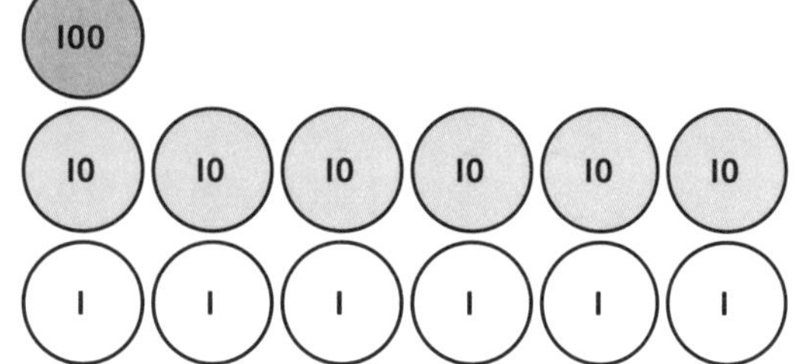

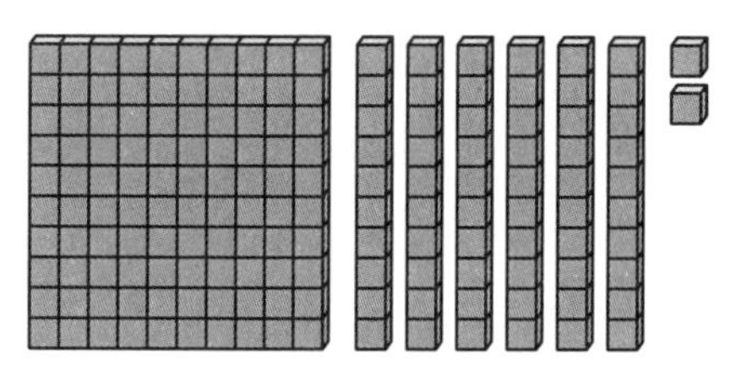

196 – 33   378 – 61   101 + 34   41 + 125

33 + 342   399 – 21   177 – 15

3 Complete the calculations. Invent another for the pattern in each column.

111 + 11 = ☐	123 + 11 = ☐	987 – 11 = ☐
111 + 22 = ☐	123 + 22 = ☐	987 – ☐ = 965
111 + 33 = ☐	123 + ☐ = 156	987 – ☐ = 954
111 + 55 = ☐	123 + ☐ = 178	☐ – 55 = 932
☐ + ☐ = ☐	☐ + ☐ = ☐	☐ – ☐ = ☐

4 Complete the calculations.

	H	T	O
	1	5	3
+		4	2

	H	T	O
	8	5	8
–		3	5

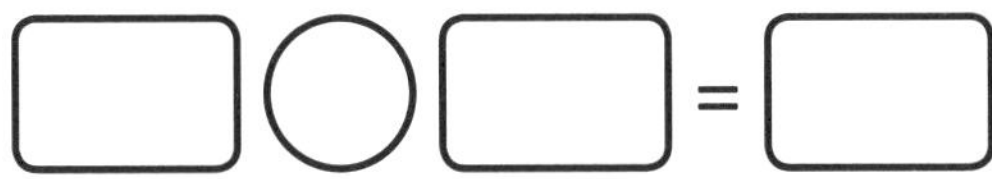

☐ ◯ ☐ = ☐

5 Fill in the missing digits and write the calculations in full.

CHALLENGE

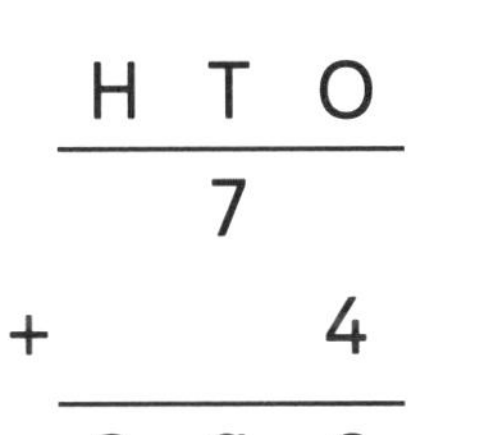

	H	T	O
		7	
+			4
	2	9	6

	H	T	O
	6		8
–		3	
		4	6

Reflect

Convince your partner that 453 + 41 = 494 and 453 – 41 = 412

→ Textbook 3A p88

Adding a 3-digit and a 2-digit number

a) The other sunflower is 23 cm taller.

What is its height?

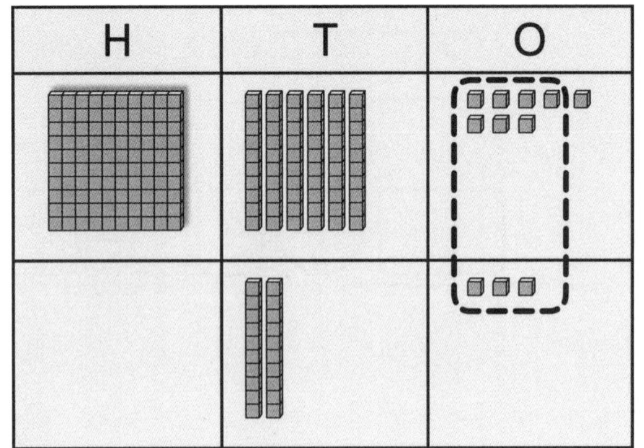

H	T	O
I	6	8
+	2	3

I68 cm tall

I68 + 23 = ☐

The other sunflower is ☐ cm tall.

b) A sunflower is I83 cm tall. It grows 5I cm taller. How tall is it now?

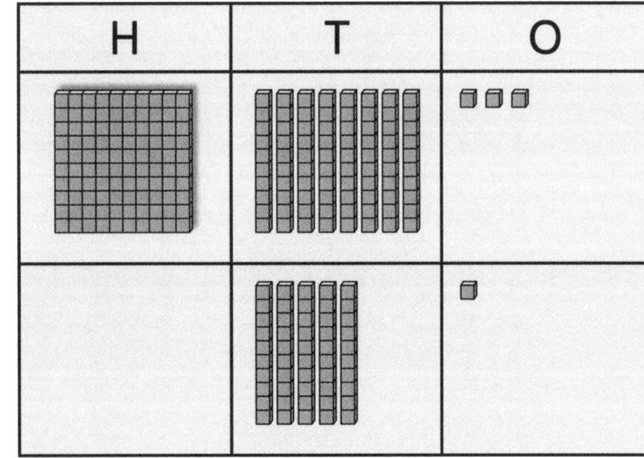

H	T	O
I	8	3
+		

I83 + ☐ = ☐

Now it is ☐ cm tall.

2 Complete this addition.

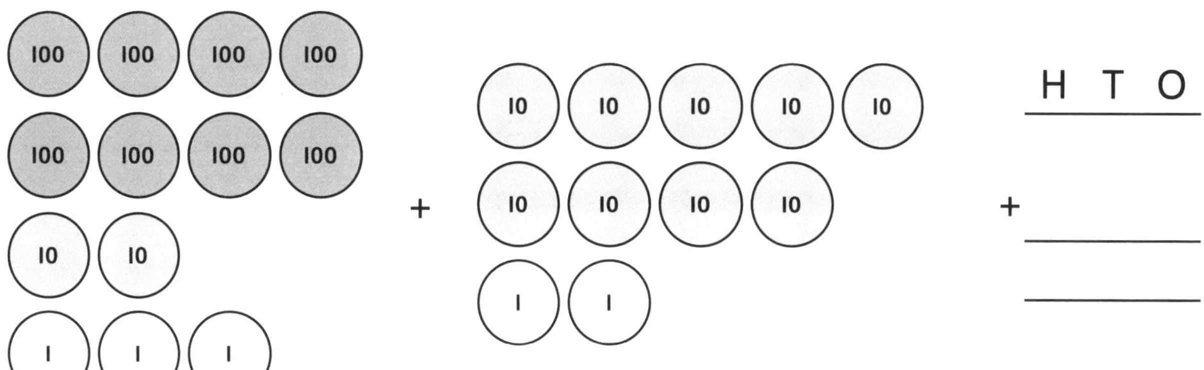

	H	T	O
+			

3 Sort the calculations into three groups.

238 + 71   827 + 31   712 + 38   327 + 18

318 + 72   731 + 28   73 + 182   28 + 137

No exchange	Exchange 10 ones	Exchange 10 tens

4 Complete these additions.

a)

	H	T	O
	2	5	8
+		4	7

c)

	H	T	O
	3	0	3
+		1	7

e)

	H	T	O
	5	2	5
+		7	6

b) 188 + 13 = ☐

d) 50 + 672 = ☐

f) ☐ = 39 + 461

5 Find the missing digits. 

a) 3☐5 + 6☐ = 416

b) 35☐ + ☐2 = 416

6 Use each number once. Write additions so that they all have to exchange 10 ones and 10 tens.

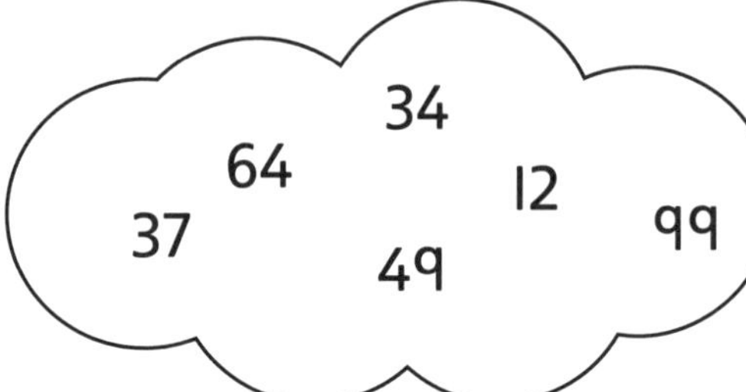

☐☐ + ☐☐☐☐

☐☐ + ☐☐☐☐

☐☐ + ☐☐☐☐

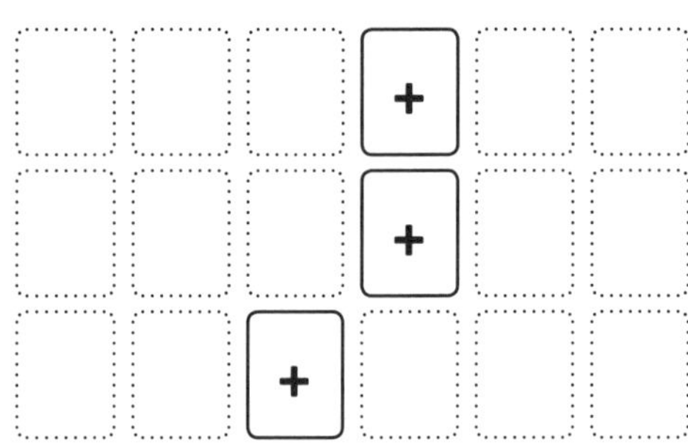

I chose the six pairs by

____

____

Reflect

Explain how to add a 3-digit and a 2-digit number in three steps.

- Step 1: ______________________________
- Step 2: ______________________________
- Step 3: ______________________________

→ Textbook 3A p92

Subtracting a 2-digit number from a 3-digit number

1 There are 345 children at school on Thursday.

a) A minibus takes 27 children on a trip. How many children are left in school?

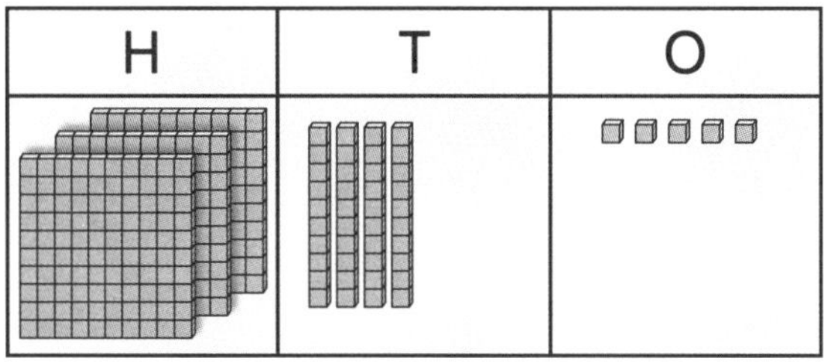

H	T	O

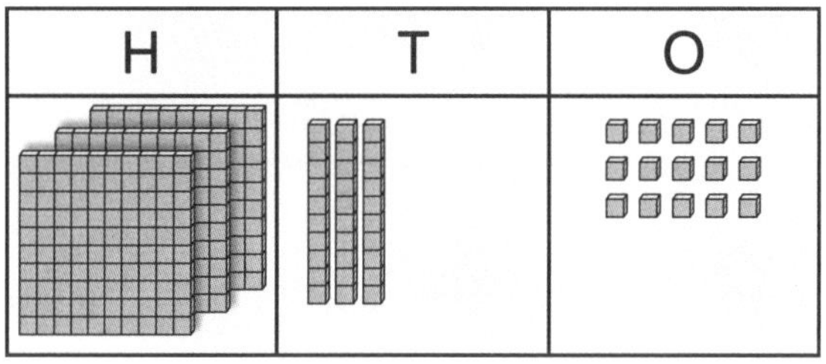

	H	T	O
	3	4	5
−		2	7

H	T	O

345 − 27 = ☐

There are ☐ children left in school.

b) On Friday there are 345 children at school. 54 children have packed lunch. The rest have school dinners. How many school dinners is that?

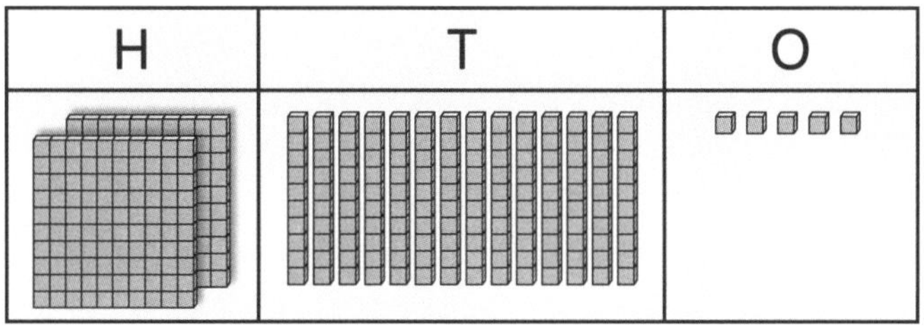

H	T	O

	H	T	O
−		5	4

345 − 54 = ☐

☐ children have school dinners.

2 Find 66 less than each number shown. 

a)

H	T	O
–	6	6

3 | 4 | 7

b)

H	T	O
–	6	6

4 | 5 | 6

3 Complete these subtractions.

a)

	H	T	O
	1	7	3
–		4	5

c)

	H	T	O
	2	6	0
–		7	6

b) 231 – 62 = ☐

d) 988 – 99 = ☐

4 Use each digit card once to make a subtraction. Find five different solutions and mark the results on the number line.

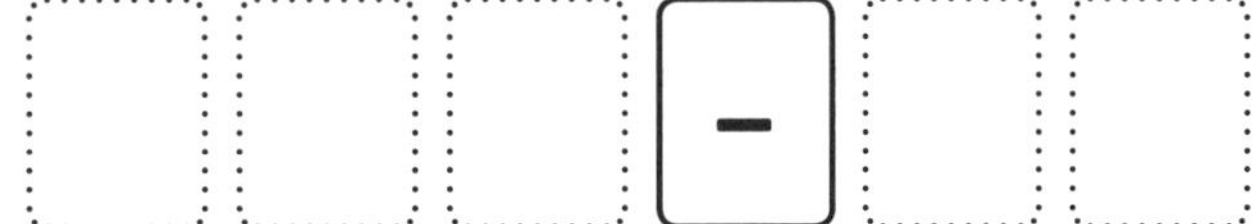

☐ ☐ ☐ – ☐ ☐

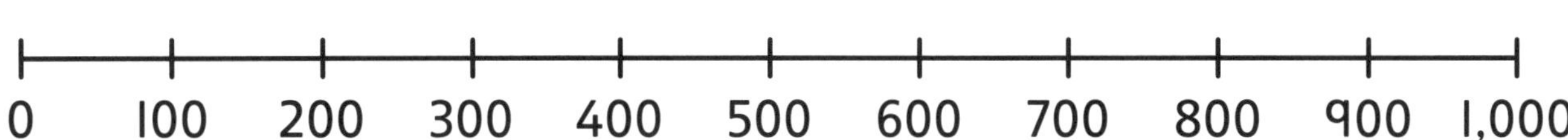

5 Find and correct the mistake in the subtraction. 

157 – 38 = ☐

	H	T	O
	1	5	7
–		3	8
	1	2	1

	H	T	O
–		3	8

6 Crack the code. Each symbol represents one digit.

	H	T	O
	△	■	△
–		△	■
	■	△	1

■ = ☐

△ = ☐

Reflect

There have been ten lessons in this unit. Think about what you learnt. What are the three most important things to remember?

1. ______

2. ______

3. ______

My favourite lesson was ______

→ Textbook 3A p96

End of unit check

My journal

What is the same and what is different about these methods for solving the subtraction 541 – 78?

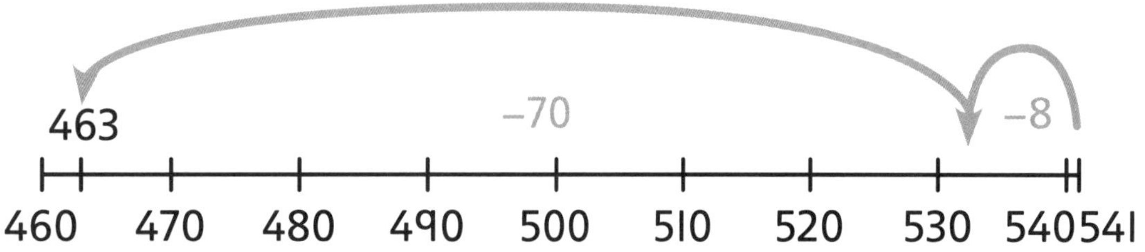

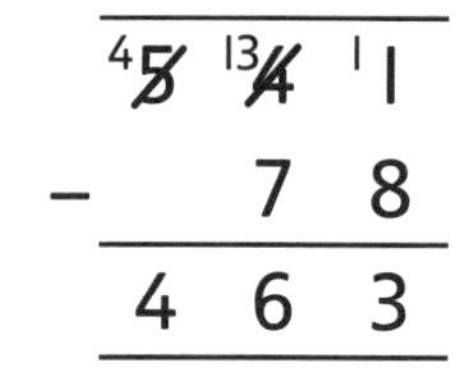

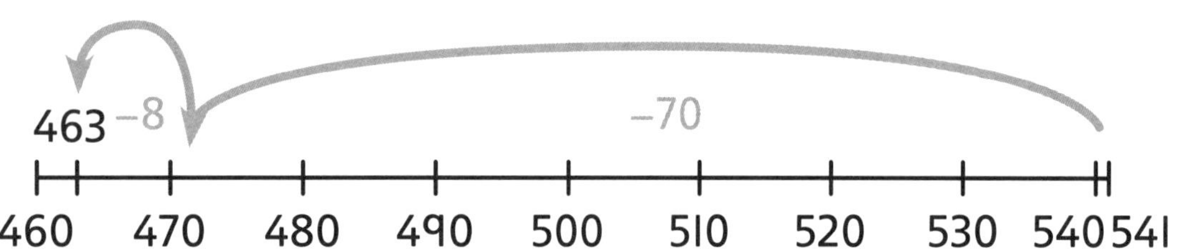

Power check

How do you feel about your work in this unit?   

Power play

Mo is thinking of a 3-digit number.

Kate is thinking of a 2-digit number.

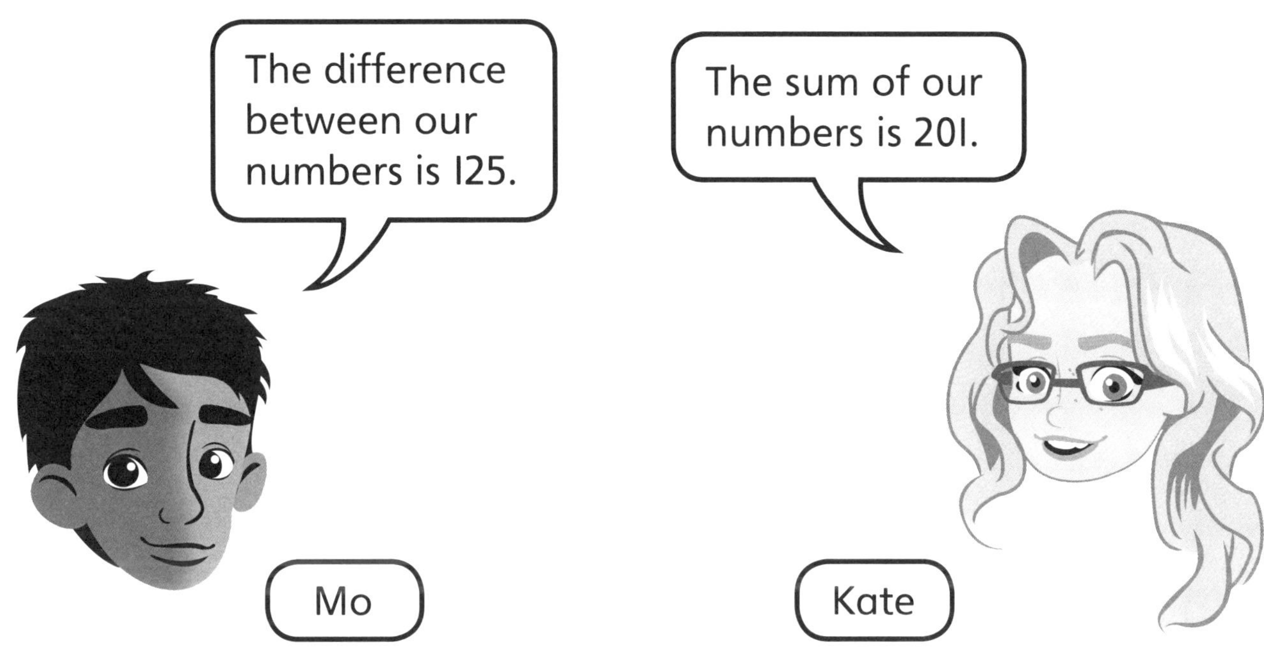

Try to find their two numbers. You may need to try a few examples and use trial and improve.

Keep a record of each attempt you make.

Create a similar puzzle for your partner to solve.
What if the difference was 250 and the sum was 402?

→ Textbook 3A p100

Addition and subtraction patterns

1 Complete these additions.

a) 254 + 4 = [ ]

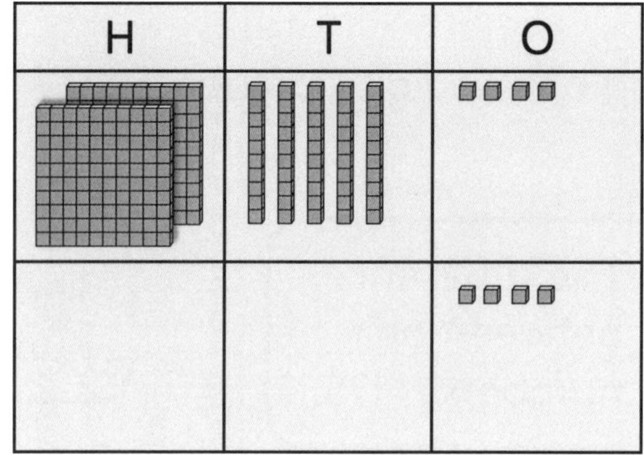

H T O
+

b) 254 + [ ] = [ ]

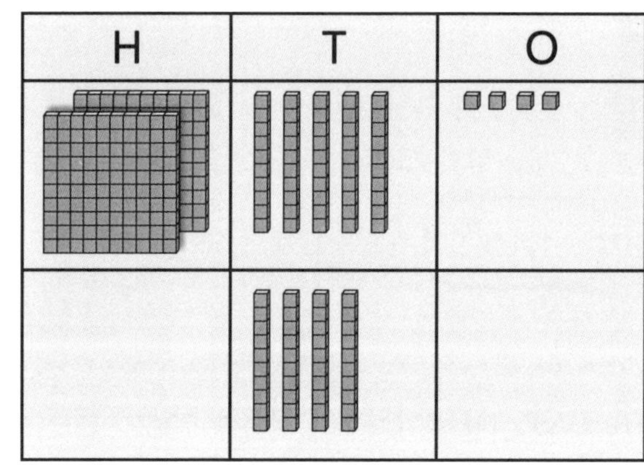

H T O
+

c) [ ] + 400 = [ ]

H T O

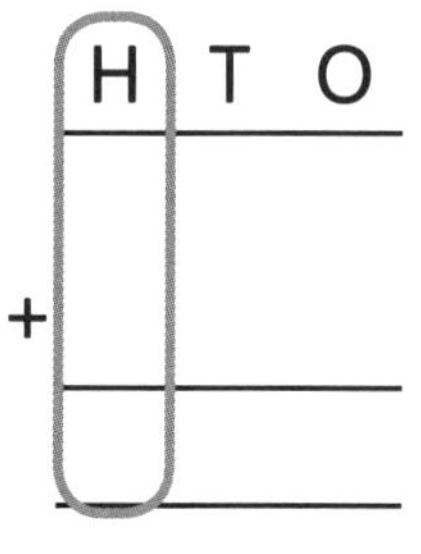

2 Complete the missing parts of these calculations.

a) 456 – 200 = ☐

H	T	O

H	T	O
4	5	6
–		

b) 456 – ☐ = 426

H	T	O

H	T	O
4	5	6
–		
4	2	6

3 Zac put the same number into each machine. The outputs were 791, 737 and 197. What number did Zac put into the machines?

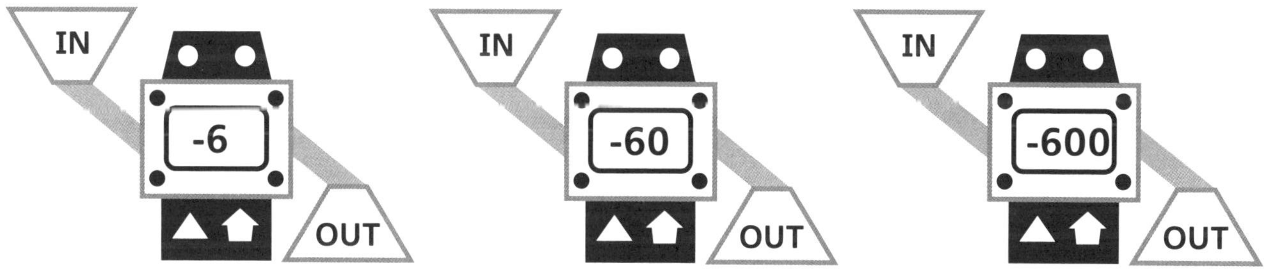

The number was ☐

4 Complete these calculations.

a) 345 + 200 = ☐

345 + 20 = ☐

345 + 2 = ☐

b) ☐ = 777 – 20

☐ = 777 – 2

777 = ☐ – 200

c) 444 + ☐ = 474

444 + ☐ = 744

444 + ☐ = 447

d) 111 = 311 ◯ ☐

111 = 411 ◯ ☐

511 = 111 ◯ ☐

5 Explain the mistake Dexter has made.

232 + 20   212 − 200

292 + 20   322 − 90

922 − 200   292 − 20

322 + 90

____

____

Reflect

Show how you would work out 654 – 300 and 654 + 300.

____

____

____

→ Textbook 3A p104

Adding two 3-digit numbers 

1 Complete these additions.

a)

H	T	O

	H	T	O
		2	
+	5	4	

b)

H	T	O

	H	T	O
+			

c)

H	T	O

	H	T	O
+			
	7	4	8

Some of the information is missing from the final place value grid.

2 Complete these additions. Try to do the last two mentally.

a)

	H	T	O
	3	4	2
+	4	5	6

b)

	H	T	O
	2	6	0
+	7	1	2

c)

	H	T	O
	3	7	4
+		2	3

d) 311 + 583 = [ ]

e) 400 + 425 = [ ]

3 There are 235 boys and 312 girls in the school.

How many children are there in total?

4 Complete these additions.

a)

	H	T	O
	1	8	6
+	3		
	4	9	8

b)

	H	T	O
	3		0
+		4	
	5	4	5

c) 548 + [ ] = 678

5 Each of these symbols is used instead of a digit. Work out what digit each symbol is showing.

	H	T	O
	4	■	★
+	◀	■	1
	★	★	7

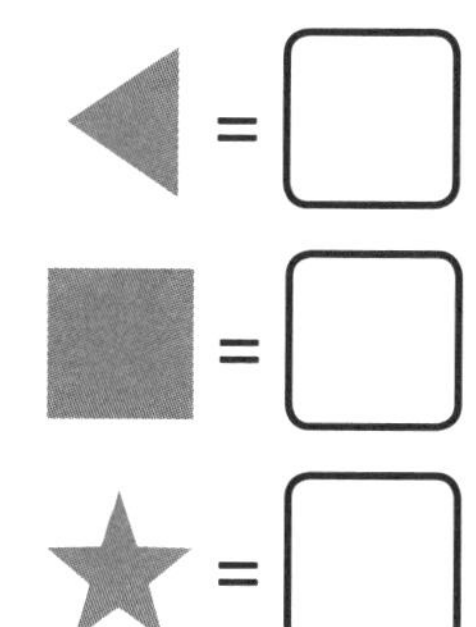

◀ = ☐

■ = ☐

★ = ☐

6 **a)** Work out 540 + 321.

	H	T	O
	5	4	0
+	3	2	1

b) Use your answer to work out the following additions.

540 + 322 = ☐

540 + 331 = ☐

540 + 421 = ☐

321 + 540 = ☐

550 + 321 = ☐

☐ = 550 + 332

I wonder if there is a quick way to work these out.

Reflect

Joe has tried to add 454 and 134.

Explain the mistakes he has made.

	H	T	O
	4	5	4
+	1	4	3
	6	9	7

→ Textbook 3A 108

Adding two 3-digit numbers 2

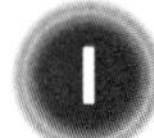

a) There are 154 boys and 168 girls at school on Monday. How many children are there altogether?

H	T	O

H	T	O
1	5	4
+ 1	6	8

154 + 168 = ☐

There are ☐ children altogether.

b) On Tuesday there are 151 boys and 163 girls at school. How many children are there altogether?

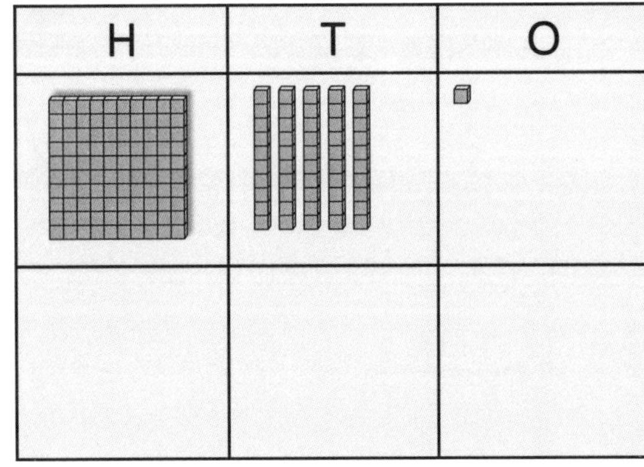

H	T	O
+		

There are ☐ children altogether.

2 **a)** Join the calculations to the bubbles to show if an exchange is needed and then complete the calculations.

H	T	O
2	3	6
+ 1	5	5

H	T	O
2	3	7
+ 1	7	3

H	T	O
3	4	7
+ 2	7	0

H	T	O
4	1	0
+ 1	9	9

H	T	O
1	0	9
+ 1	9	0

H	T	O
	8	8
+ 1	1	3

No exchange needed

Exchange 10 ones for 1 ten

Exchange 10 tens for 1 hundred

b) Do any of the calculations join to more than one bubble?

3 **a)** Write the missing digits. 

H	T	O
4	3	2
+		
9	1	9

H	T	O
1	7	
+	1	3
1	9	1

H	T	O
	2	
+ 2		2
9	1	1

b) Find three different solutions.

H	T	O
		9
+ 1		
9	1	1

H	T	O
		9
+ 1		
9	1	1

H	T	O
		9
+ 1		
9	1	1

Use each card once in each calculation. Make totals greater than 900.

5 5 8

How many solutions can you find?

H	T	O
4		
+ 4		

H	T	O
4		
+ 4		

H	T	O
4		
+ 4		

H	T	O
4		
+ 4		

H	T	O
4		
+ 4		

H	T	O
4		
+ 4		

Can you find all the possible solutions? Are there any more?

Reflect

Bella is working out 305 + 407. She thinks the answer will have 0 in the tens column because there are no 10s in 305 or 407.

Explain Bella's mistake.

Subtracting a 3-digit number from a 3-digit number 1

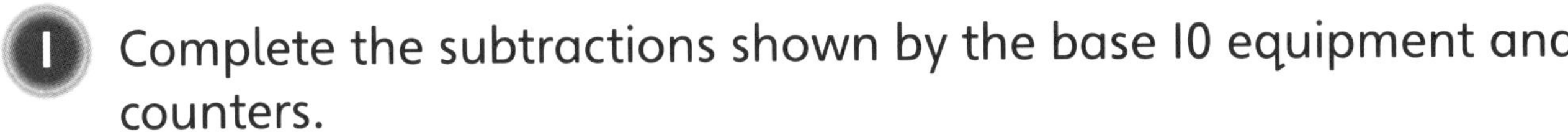

1 Complete the subtractions shown by the base 10 equipment and counters.

a) 678 – 135 = ☐

H	T	O

	H	T	O
	6	7	8
–	1	3	5

b) 876 – 351 = ☐

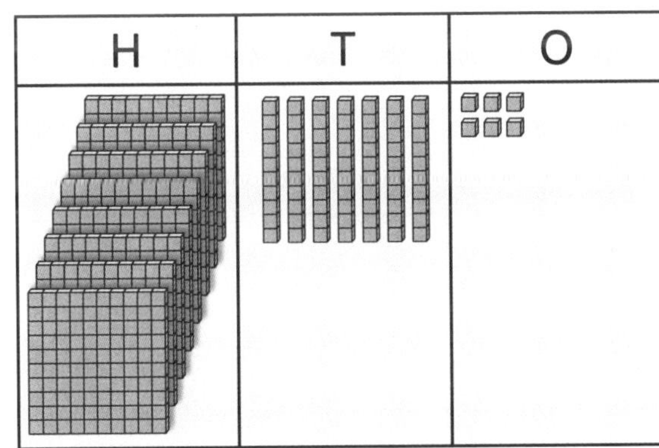

	H	T	O
–			

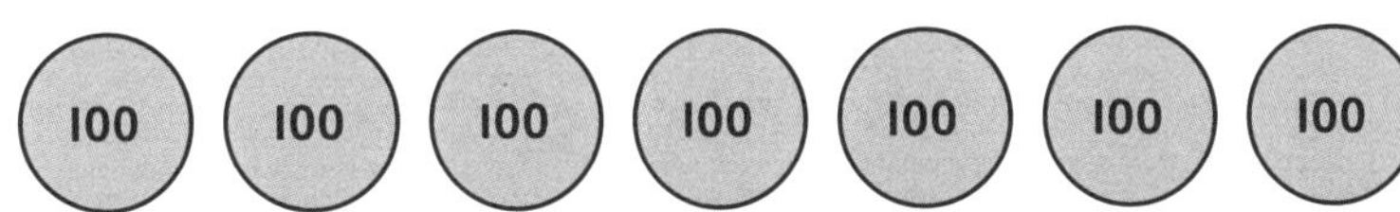

c) ☐ – 531 = ☐

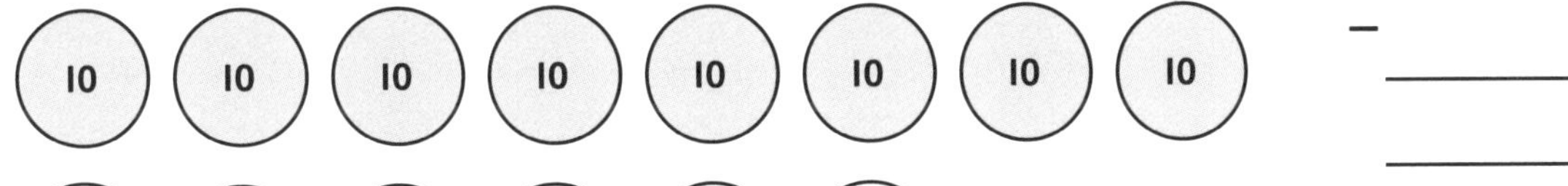

10 10 10 10 10 10 10 10

	H	T	O
–			

2 There were 377 people at the cinema and 599 people at a concert.

How many more people were at the concert?

H	T	O
–		

☐ more people were at the concert.

3 **a)** Complete these subtractions.

888 – 434 = ☐

	H	T	O
	8	8	8
–	4	3	4

868 – 443 = ☐

	H	T	O
	8	6	8
–			

688 – 340 = ☐

	H	T	O
–			

688 – 34 = ☐

	H	T	O
–			

b) Try to use a mental method to solve these subtractions.

886 – 340 = ☐

☐ = 668 – 304

4 **a)** Find the missing digits from this subtraction.

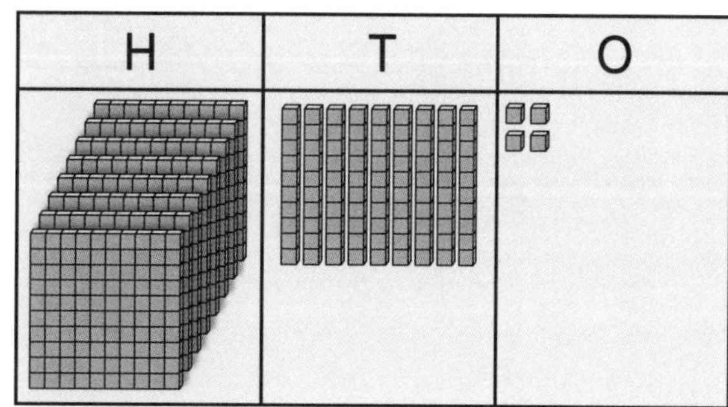

	H	T	O
	8	9	4
–			
	2	0	4

b) Think of a subtraction. Write a word problem that can be solved using your subtraction.

5 Use only the digits 0, 1 and 2 to complete each subtraction. Find two solutions to each.

a) The answer is between 200 and 220.

333 – ☐☐☐   333 – ☐☐☐

b) The answer is odd.

444 – ☐☐☐   444 – ☐☐☐

c) The answer is a multiple of 5.

☐☐☐ – 101   

Reflect

Show how to solve 372 – 251 using equipment or a drawing.

→ Textbook 3A p116

Subtracting a 3-digit number from a 3-digit number 2

1 **a)** 513 people were invited to a party. 181 did not come.

How many people came to the party?

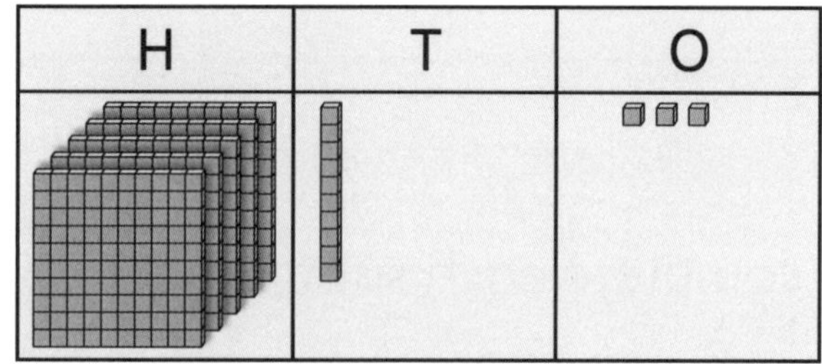

	H	T	O
	5	1	3
−	1	8	1

H	T	O

b) There were 385 people at the disco. There were 169 people at the fair.

How many more people were at the disco?

H	T	O

	H	T	O
−			

2 Complete these calculations.

543 − 235 = ☐ 543 − 345 = ☐ ☐ = 508 − 91

	H	T	O
	5	4	3
−			

	H	T	O
−			

3 Solve the subtractions.

a) 340 – 187

H	T	O
–		

b) 304 – 187

H	T	O
–		

c) 400 – 178

H	T	O
–		

4 Complete the column subtractions.

a)

H	T	O

	H	T	O
	5	7	5
–			
	1	3	6

b)

	H	T	O
			0
–	5	3	
	3	9	1

5 What subtraction is Reena trying to work out?

Write it as a column subtraction.

H	T	O
100 100 100	10 10 10 10 10 10 10 10 10	1 1 1 1 1 1 1 1 1 1 1 1 1 1 1

	H	T	O
–			

6 Read these ideas.

Test the ideas and describe what you notice.

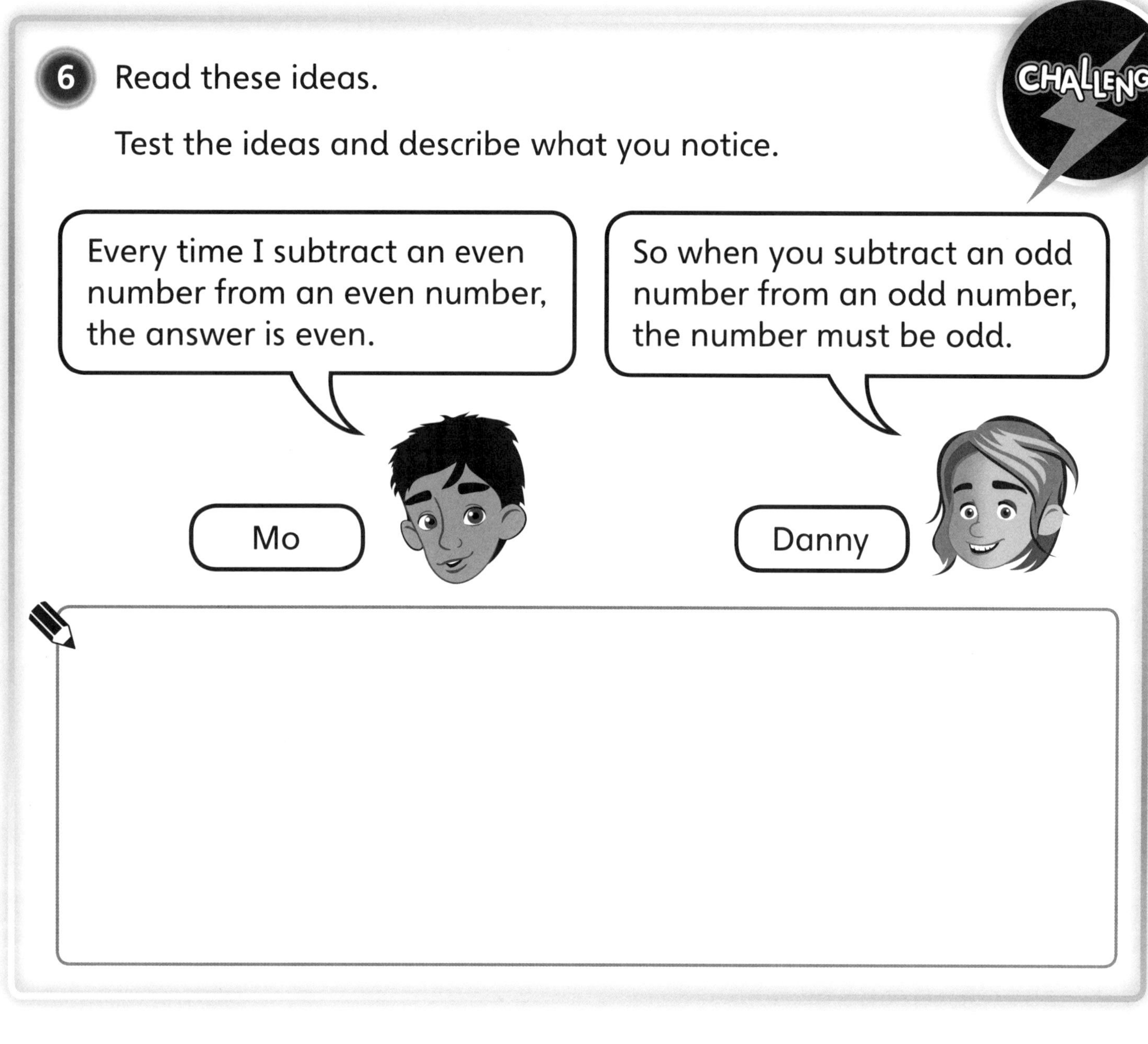

Reflect

Write a calculation that needs one exchange only. How do you know?

→ Textbook 3A p120

Estimating answers to additions and subtractions

1 Draw arrows to show approximately where each number should appear on the number line.

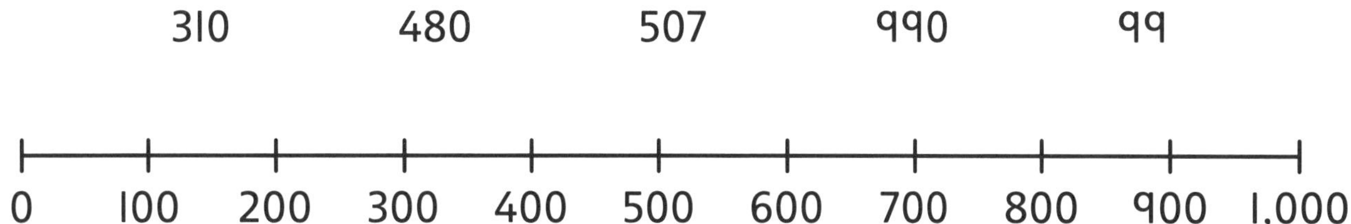

2 Choose numbers to complete each sentence.

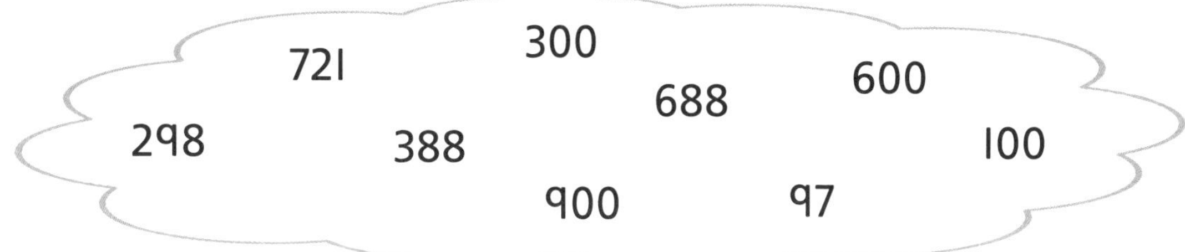

[ ] is approximately 400.

[ ] is approximately 700.

590 is approximately [ ].

904 is approximately [ ].

[ ] is approximately [ ].

[ ] is approximately [ ].

3 Complete estimates for each calculation.

a) 311 + 188

My estimate:

[ ]00 + [ ]00 = [ ]00

311 + 188 is approximately [ ].

b) 607 – 411

My estimate:

[ ] – [ ] = [ ]

607 – 411 is approximately [ ].

Sort these calculations into the table by estimating.

195 + 304   901 – 99   548 – 351

990 – 195   949 – 452   88 + 399

Approximately 200	Approximately 500	Approximately 800

One of the children has made a mistake. Use estimates to decide which calculation should be redone.

a)

	H	T	O
	${}^{4}\not{5}$	${}^{10}\not{1}$	${}^{1}2$
–	2	8	9
	2	2	3

Estimate ______________

b)

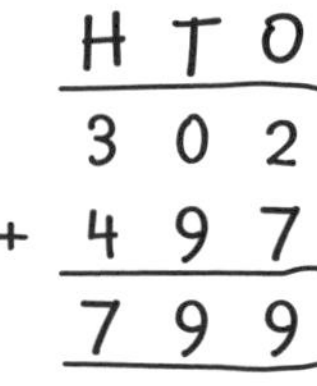

Estimate ______________

c)

	H	T	O
	7	8	1
–	3	9	4
	3	1	3

Estimate ______________

Use your estimates to decide which calculation to redo. Complete it correctly.

CHALLENGE

6 The children are working on 198 + 297.

I think the answer must be less than 500.

Jamie

I will not know if it will be more or less than 500 until I do the calculation.

Andy

Who do you agree with?

I agree with ________________ because ______________________

____

____

Reflect

Write an estimate for each calculation and then explain your reasoning.

205 + 198   513 – 308   448 + 297

__________   __________   __________

- ____
- ____
- ____
-

→ Textbook 3A p124

Checking strategies

1 a) There is a mistake in one of these subtractions. Complete the part-whole models and write an addition to check each subtraction.

435 – 215 = 220

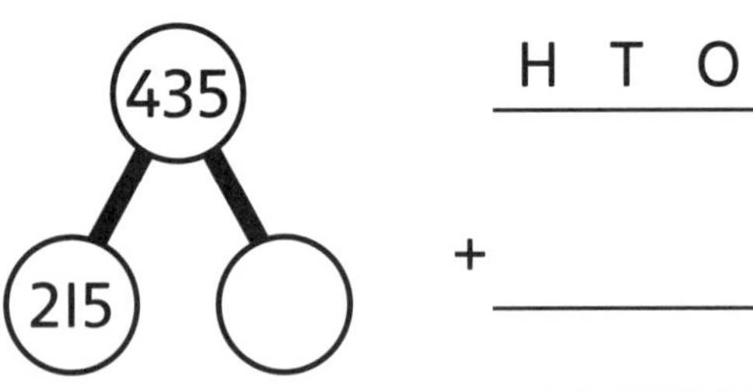

H T O

+

211 = 553 – 364

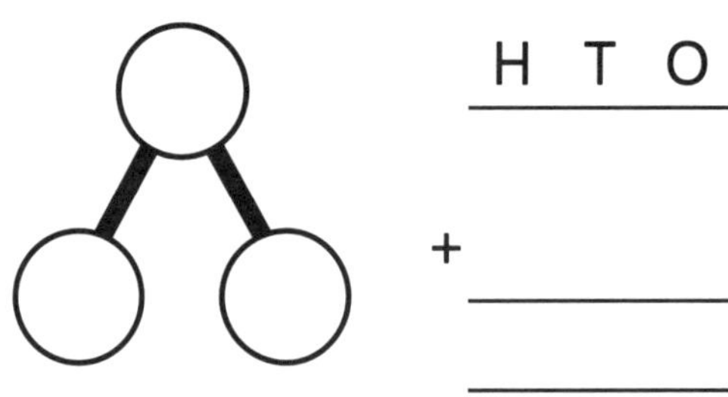

H T O

+

b) Now complete the subtraction correctly.

The correct subtraction is

H T O

–

2 Complete the part-whole model.

Write an addition to check the subtraction.

517 – 310 = 207

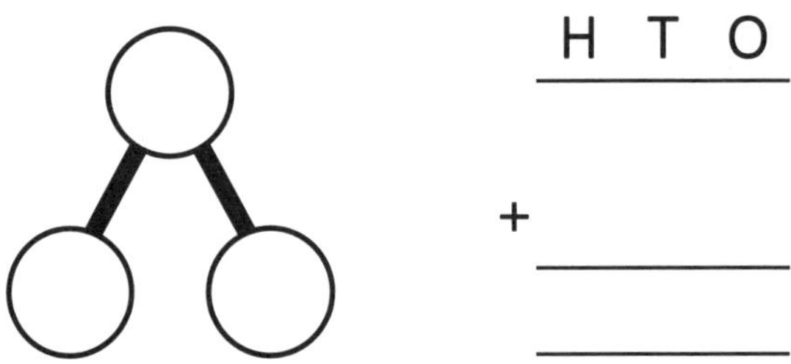

H T O

+

I think the subtraction is correct / incorrect because ______________

____

3 **a)** Write the subtraction to match Olivia's story.

Use an addition to check her working out.

H T O

\+

b) I agree / disagree with Olivia because ______________________

____

____

4 Complete the calculations using fact families.

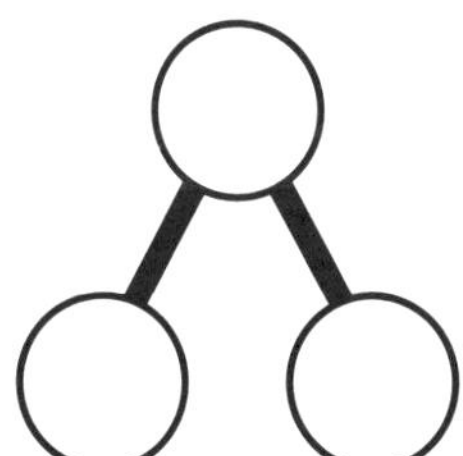

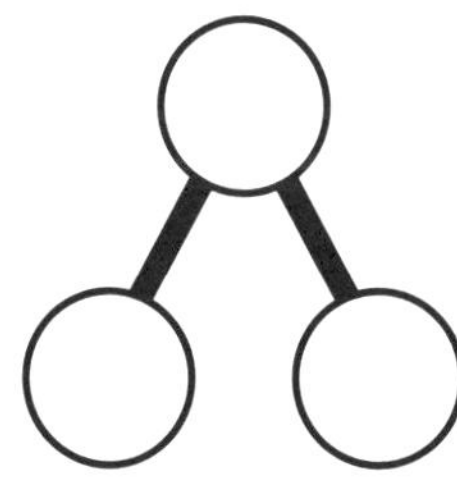

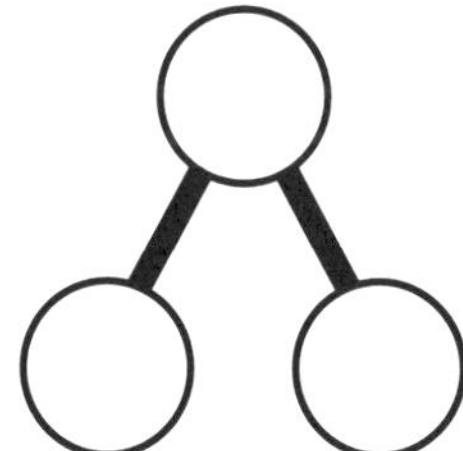

755 – 300 = ☐	200 = ☐ – 340	601 – 599 = ☐
755 – ☐ = 300	340 = ☐ – 200	599 = 601 – ☐
300 + ☐ = 755	☐ + 200 = ☐	599 + ☐ = 601
755 = ☐ + 300	200 + ☐ = ☐	601 = ☐ + 599

5 Show an addition on the number line to complete the subtraction.

700 – 499 = [ ]

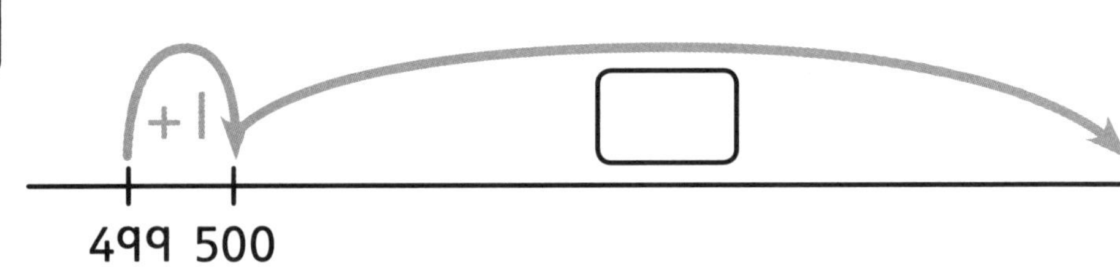

499 + [ ] = 700

6 291 – 100 = 191

Explore and explain how you can use this fact to work out:

a) 291 – 192

b) 99 + 192

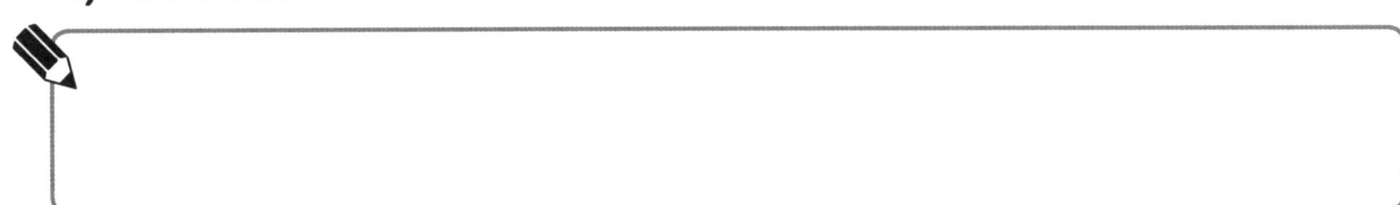

Reflect

What is the difference between these two checking strategies: using fact families and using estimation?

→ Textbook 3A p128

Problem solving – addition and subtraction 

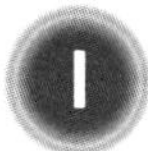 a) Class 3 raised £125 and Class 4 raised £210.

How much did they raise altogether?

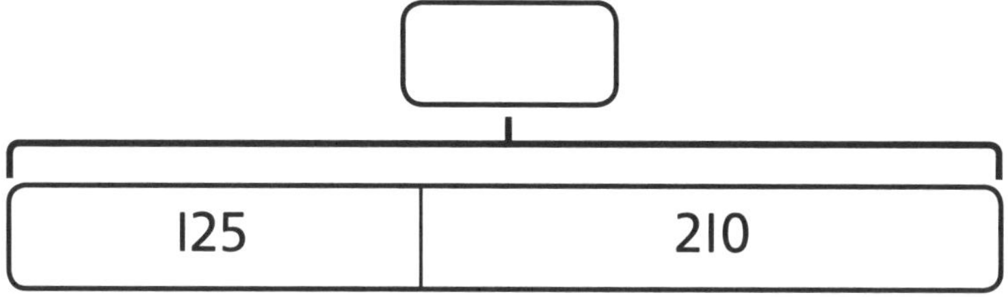

Class 3 and 4 raised £ ☐ altogether.

b) Class 5 have raised £231 so far. They are aiming for £325.

How much more do they need to raise?

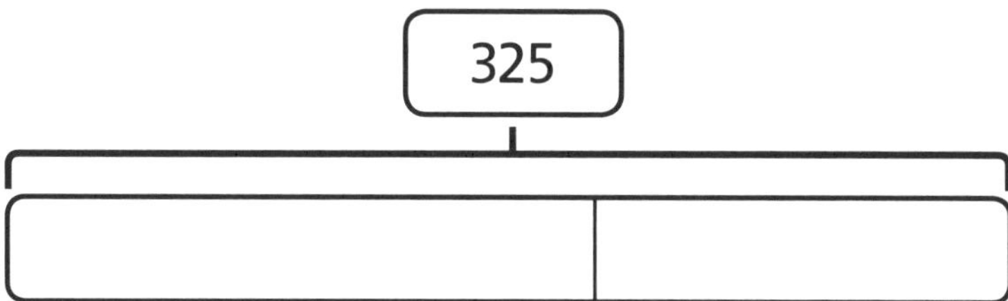

H T O

They need to raise £ ☐ more to reach their target.

2 Dana and Luis are playing a game. Dana has scored 88 points and Luis has scored 175 points.

How many have they scored altogether?

Circle the diagram that solves the solution best.

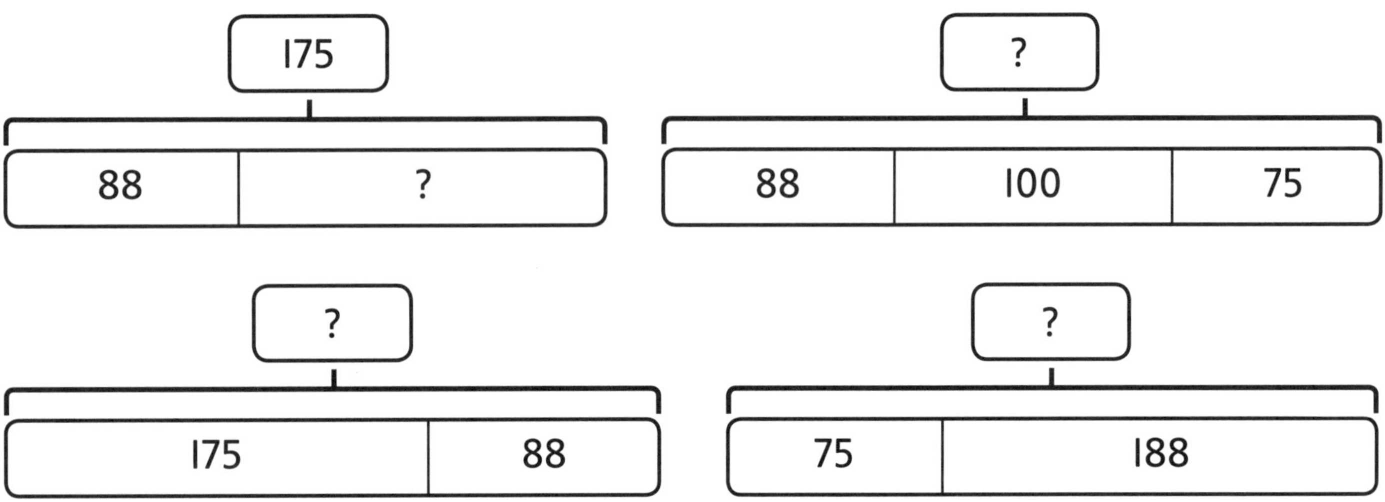

They have scored [ ] points altogether.

3 Jamie has some shells. She adds 128 shells to her collection. Now she has 266 shells.

How many did she have to begin with?

Draw a bar model to help you solve the problem.

H T O

−

Jamie had [ ] shells to begin with.

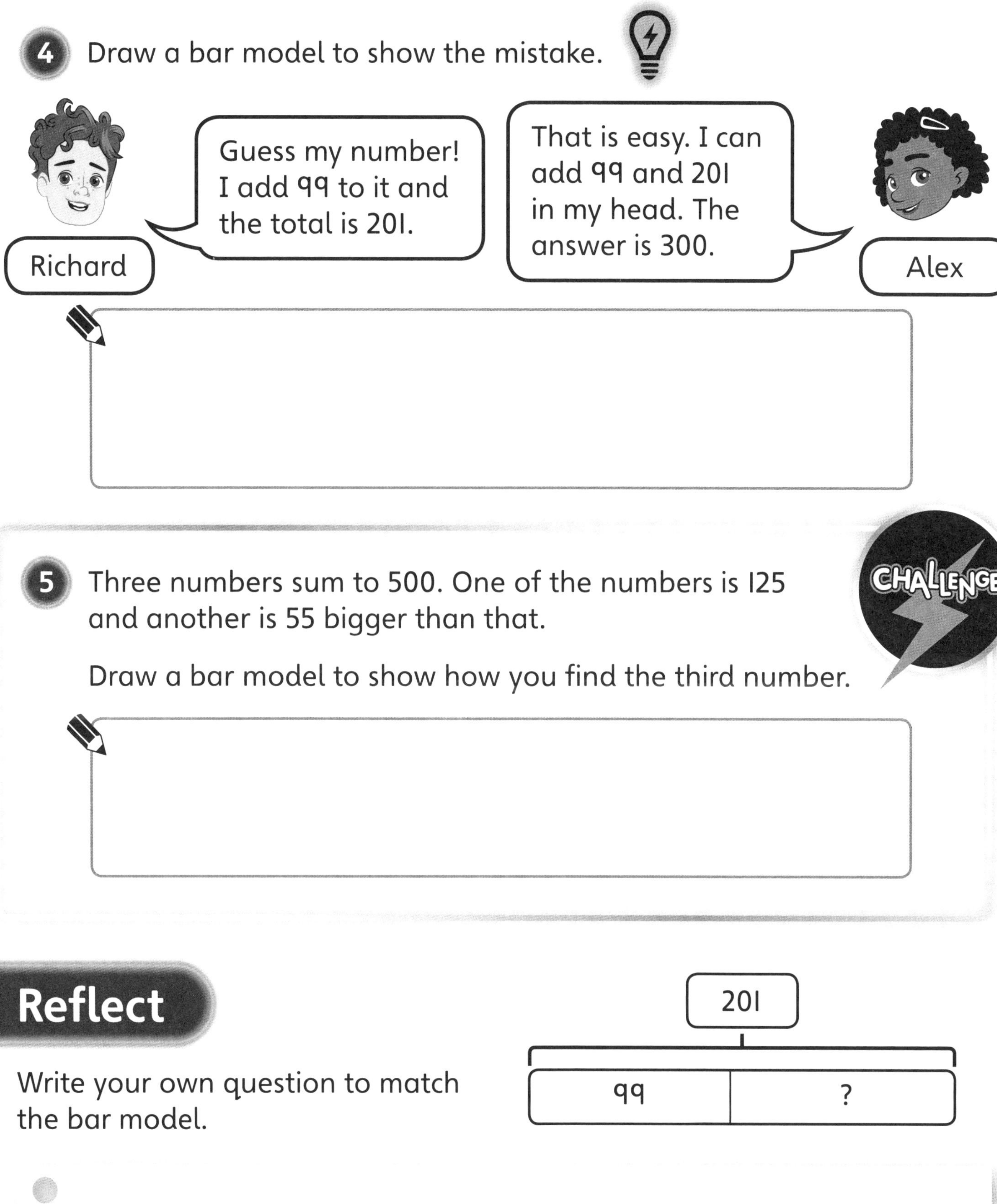

4 Draw a bar model to show the mistake.

5 Three numbers sum to 500. One of the numbers is 125 and another is 55 bigger than that.

Draw a bar model to show how you find the third number.

Reflect

Write your own question to match the bar model.

201	
99	?

→ Textbook 3A p132

Problem solving – addition and subtraction 2

1 There were 314 frogs in a pond in summer. By winter there were only 262 frogs. How many more frogs were there in the summer?

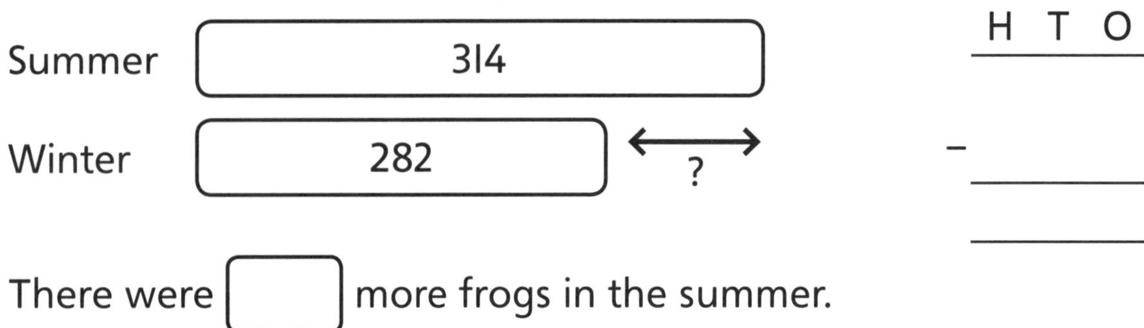

There were ☐ more frogs in the summer.

2 Daniel spent £175 on his holiday. Reena spent £205.

a) Complete the bar model to show how much more Reena spent.

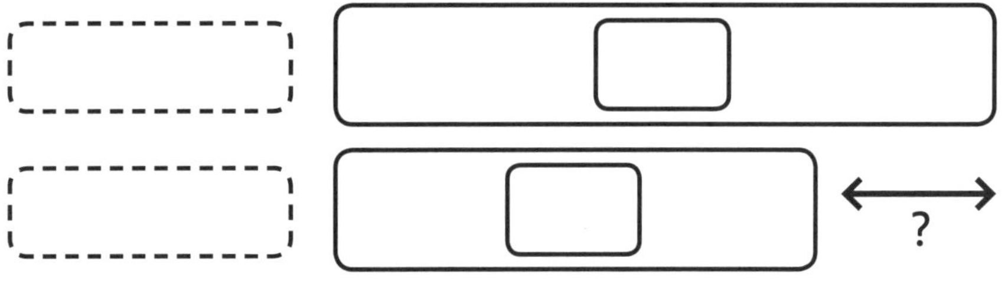

Reena spent £☐ more than Daniel.

b) How much did they spend altogether?

They spent £☐ altogether.

3 The Eiffel Tower is 324 m tall. The Blackpool Tower is 166 m shorter.

How tall is the Blackpool Tower?

Eiffel Tower [ ] m

The Blackpool Tower is [ ] m tall.

4 School A has 158 boys and 161 girls. School B has 173 boys and 118 girls.

Draw bar models to show each problem.

a) How many more girls than boys are there in School A?

b) How many more children are there in School A than in School B?

5 Ebo thought of a number. Zac thought of a different number.

Complete the bar model to work out Ebo and Zac's numbers.

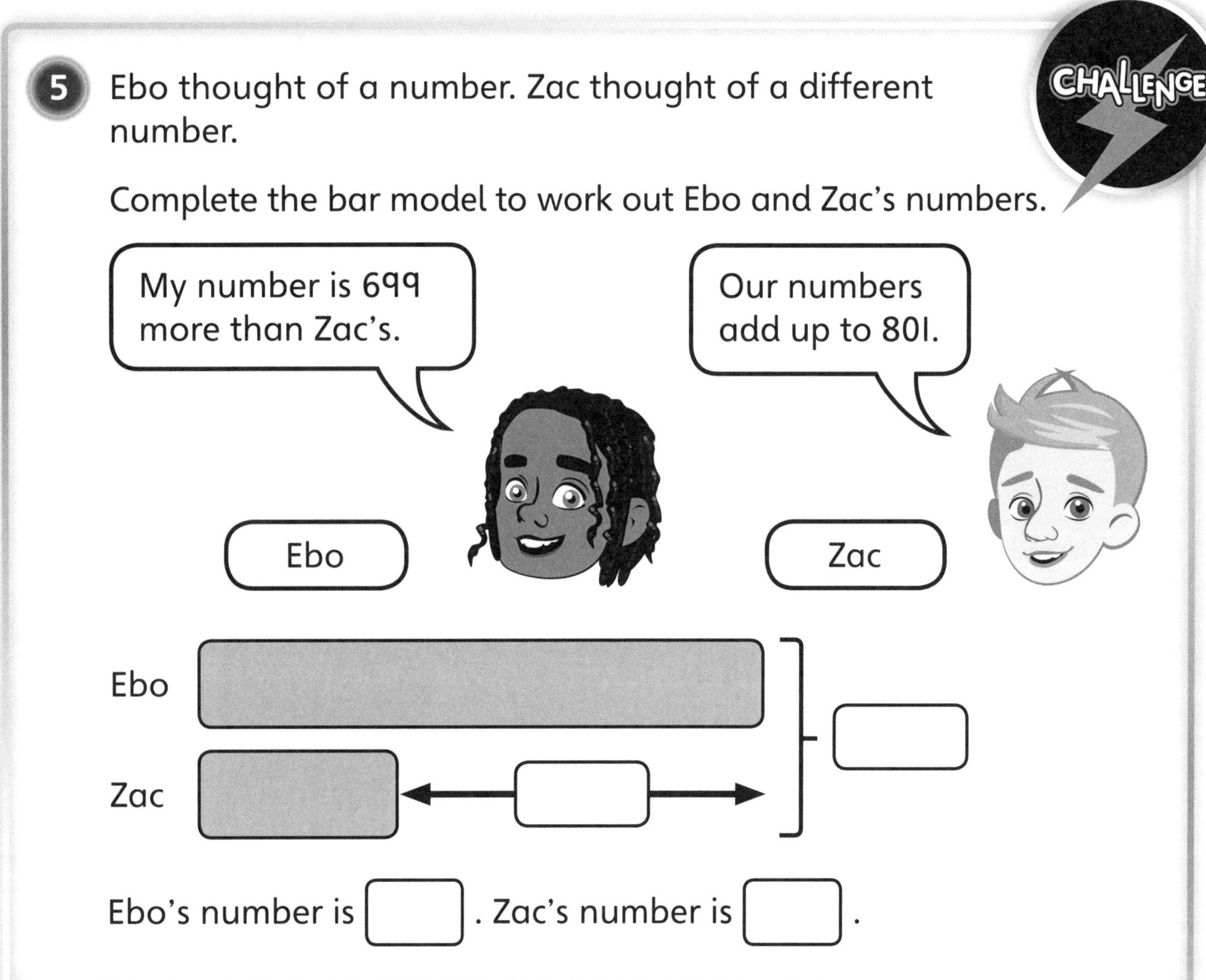

Ebo's number is [ ]. Zac's number is [ ].

Reflect

Describe when you would draw two bars and when you would draw one on a bar model.

End of unit check

My journal

Sort these calculations from easiest to hardest.

Explain your decisions.

a) 301 − 199 = ☐

b) 584 + 366 = ☐

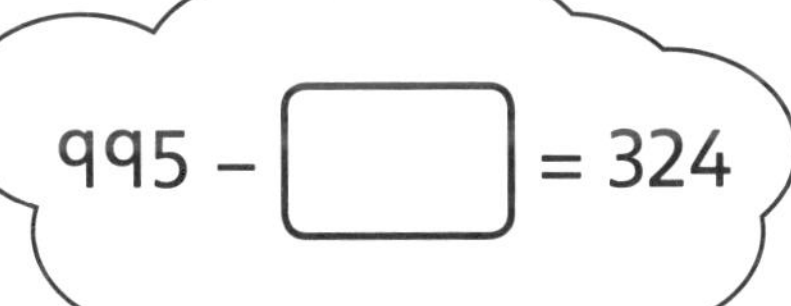

c) 995 − ☐ = 324

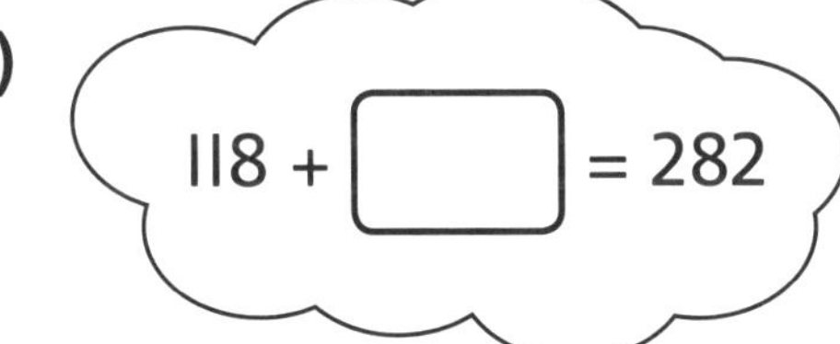

d) 118 + ☐ = 282

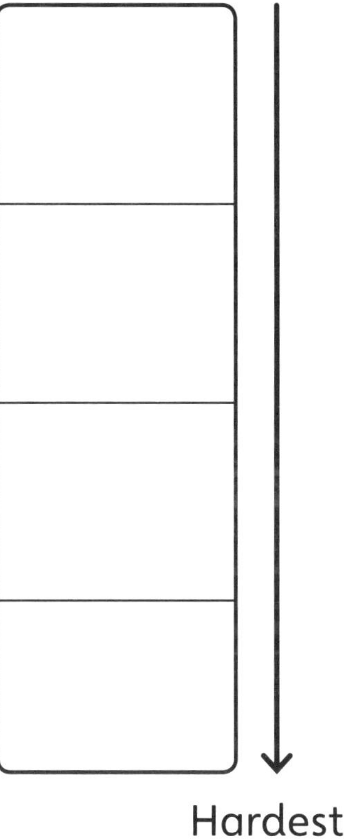

____

____

Power check

How do you feel about your work in this unit?

Power play

Take it in turns to spin a 0–5 spinner.

Write each number you spin as one digit of your own addition.

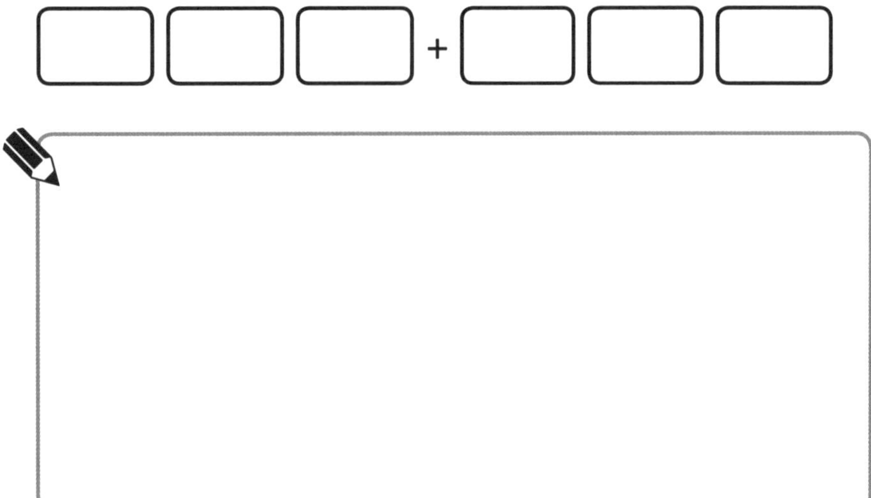

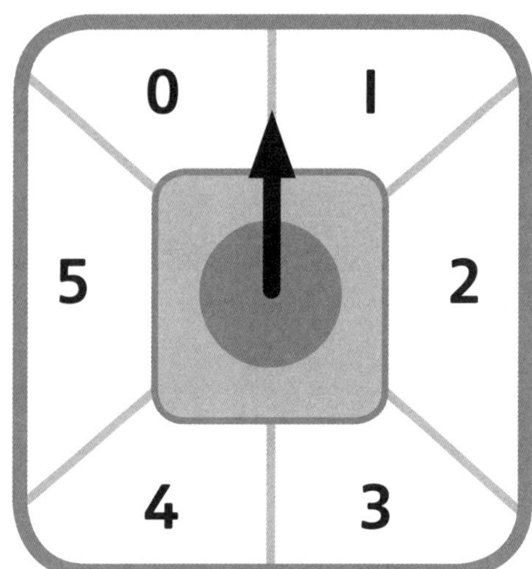

When your addition is ready to work out, find the answer and mark it on the number line.

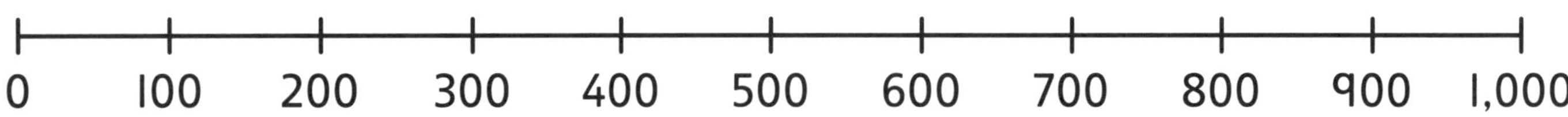

The aim is to get three answers in a row, without one of your partner's answers in between.

Change the challenge to see who can get an answer closest to a target number, such as 500.

→ Textbook 3A p140

Multiplication – equal grouping

1. Which images show equal groups?

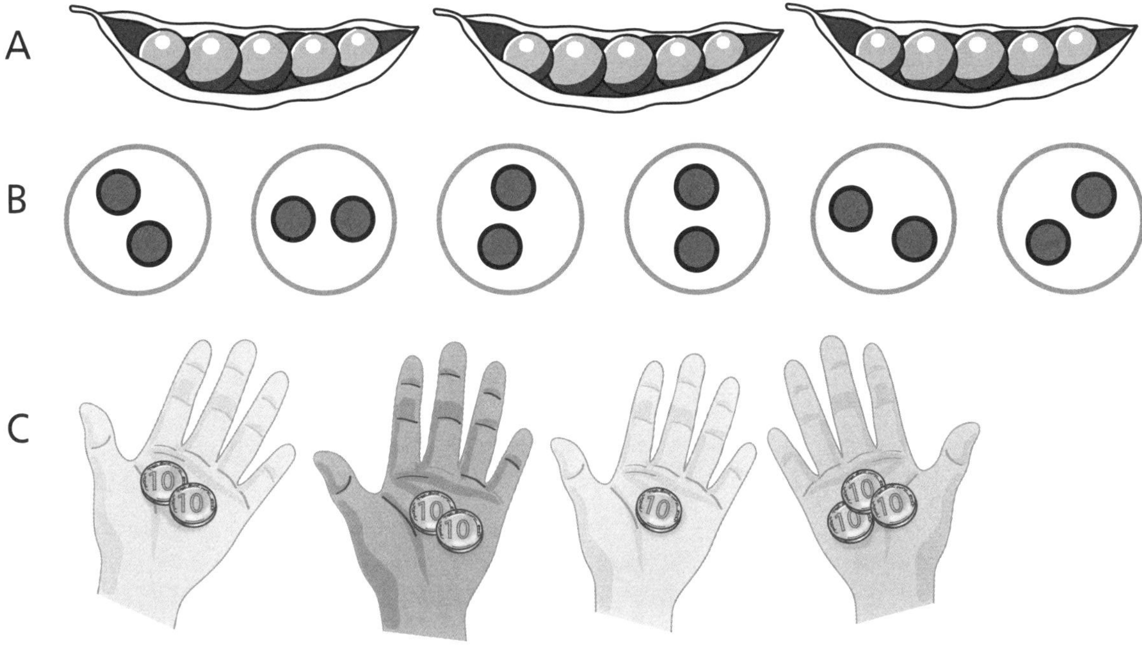

_______________ show equal groups.

2. How many acorns are there in total?

There are ☐ groups of ☐ acorns.

☐ + ☐ + ☐ = ☐

☐ × ☐ = ☐

There are ☐ acorns.

3 How many mugs are there in total?

There are [ ] groups of [ ] mugs.

[ ] + [ ] + [ ] + [ ] = [ ]

[ ] × [ ] = [ ]

There are [ ] mugs.

4 Match the repeated addition to the correct multiplication.

3 × 10	4 + 4
5 + 5 + 5 + 5 + 5 + 5	4 × 3
2 × 4	6 × 5
3 + 3 + 3 + 3	10 + 10 + 10

5 Complete the sentences to make them correct.

4 × 5 = 5 + 5 + [ ]

6 × 10 = 4 × 10 + [ ]

6 Circle the groups for each calculation.

2 groups of 6, or 2 × 6

6 groups of 2, or 6 × 2

4 groups of 3, or 4 × 3

3 groups of 4, or 3 × 4

Reflect

What multiplication statements can you see?

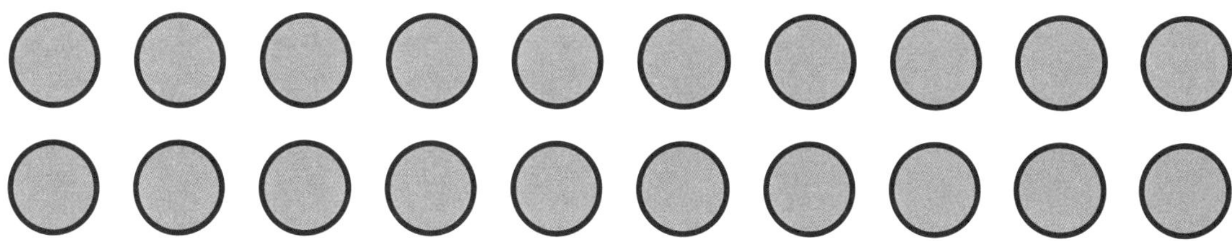

→ Textbook 3A p144

Multiplying by 3

1 **a)** How many chairs are there in total?

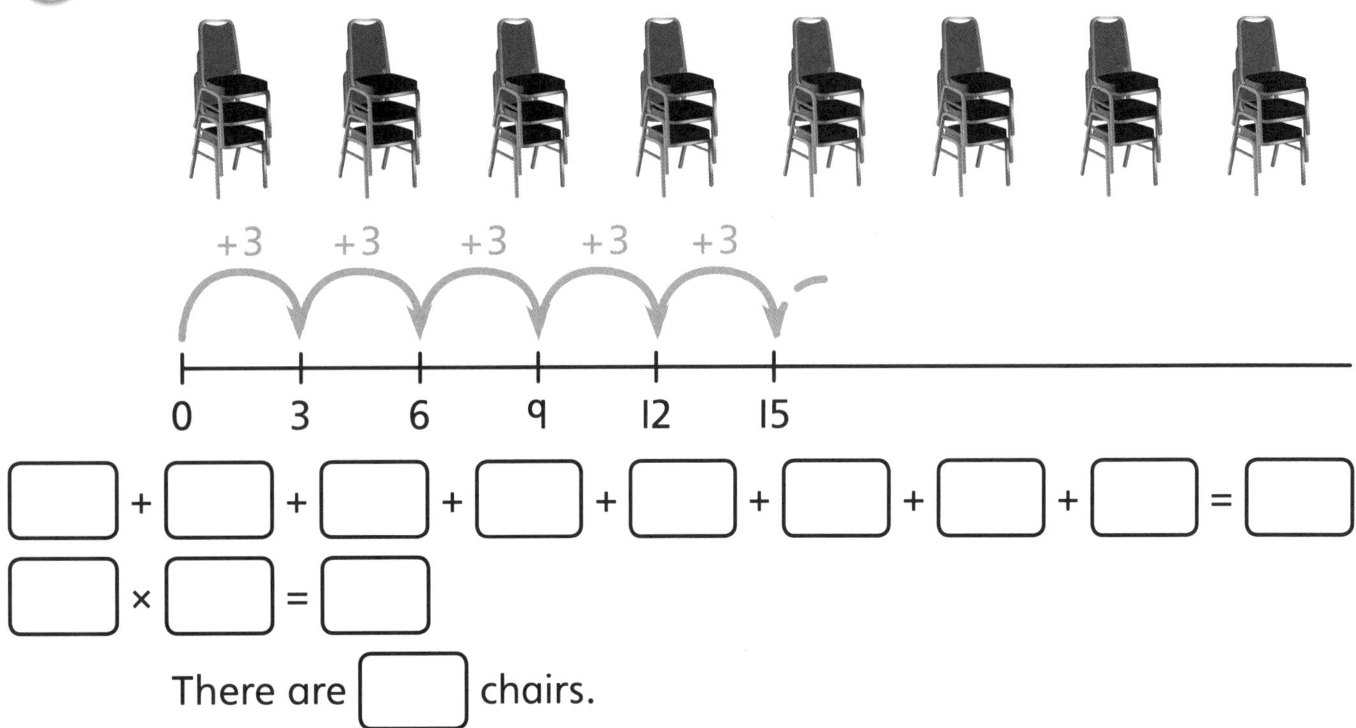

☐ + ☐ + ☐ + ☐ + ☐ + ☐ + ☐ + ☐ = ☐

☐ × ☐ = ☐

There are ☐ chairs.

b) Roses are in bunches of 3. How many roses are there in total?

☐ × ☐ = ☐

There are ☐ roses.

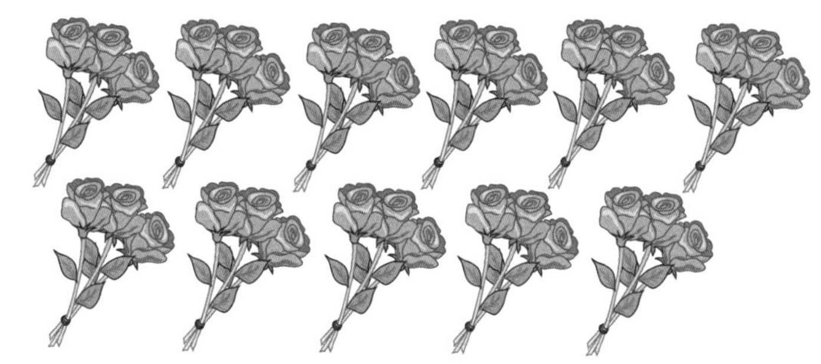

2 A box contains 3 cakes.

Richard has 6 boxes of cakes.

How many cakes does Richard have?

☐ × ☐ = ☐

Richard has ☐ cakes.

3 a) There are 12 marbles in each box.

12 Marbles | 12 Marbles | 12 Marbles

How many marbles are there in total?

☐ × ☐ = ☐

There are ☐ marbles.

b) Andy removes 2 marbles from each box.

How many marbles are there now?

☐ × ☐ = ☐

There are ☐ marbles.

4 How many counters are there in total?

I know the answer! I did it using two multiplications and then I added together.

I think there is a way of doing this with just one multiplication.

☐ × ☐ = ☐

There are ☐ counters in total.

5 12 × 3 = 36

Use this to help you work out 15 × 3.

Explain your method.

15 × 3 = ☐

6 Do you think Danny is correct? Why?

Reflect

The answer is 27. The working out is 9 × 3. What could the question be?

-
-
-

→ Textbook 3A p148

Dividing by 3

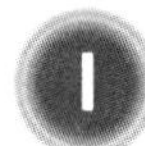

a) These grapes are shared equally between 3 children.

How many grapes does each child get?

There are ☐ grapes.

There are ☐ children.

Each child gets ☐ grapes.

b) Balloons are tied into bundles of 3.

How many bundles can be made?

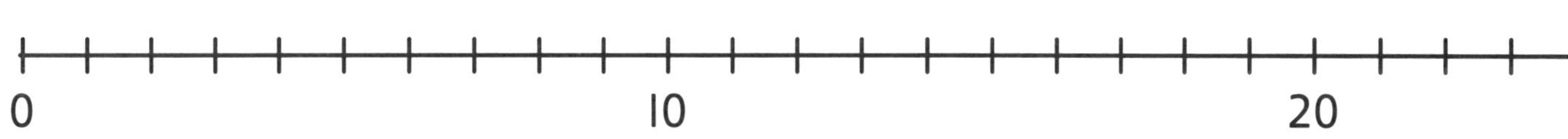

There are ☐ balloons.

There are 3 balloons in each bundle.

☐ ÷ ☐ = ☐

There are ☐ bundles.

c) 9 badges are shared equally between 3 people.

How many badges does each person get?

☐ ÷ ☐ = ☐

Each person gets ☐ badges.

2 **a)** Use the array to work out 27 ÷ 3.

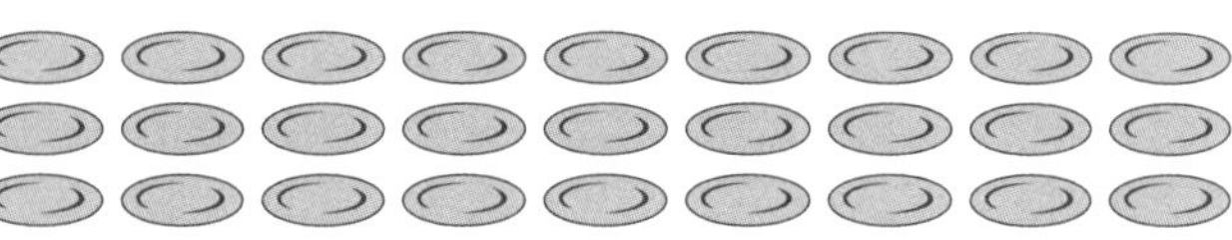

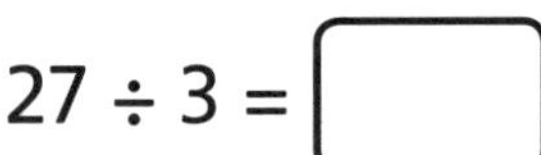

27 ÷ 3 = ☐

b) Use the array to work out 15 ÷ 3.

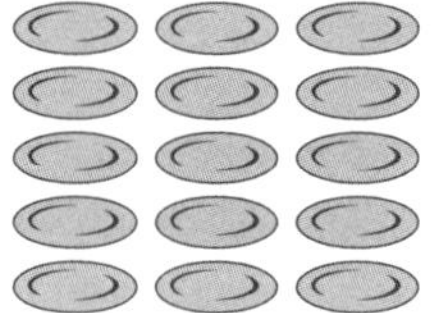

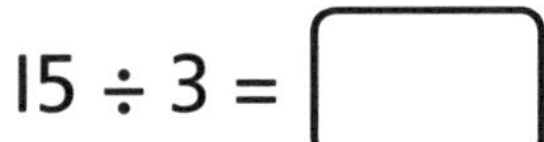

15 ÷ 3 = ☐

3 12 cubes are shared equally among 3 bags.

a) How many cubes are put into each bag?

There are ☐ cubes in each bag.

b) Can you share 13 cubes equally between 3 bags?

Explain your answer.

I don't think I can share them equally.
If I cannot, I wonder how many more I need.

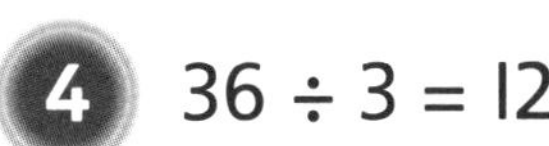

4 36 ÷ 3 = 12

What is 42 ÷ 3?

42 ÷ 3 = [ ]

I will use a number line to help. I don't think I need to start at 0 though.

5 Here are some towers of cubes.

 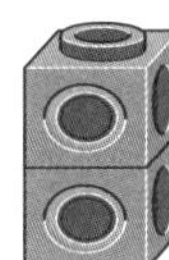 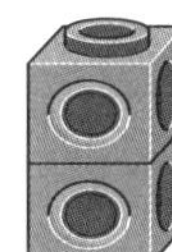 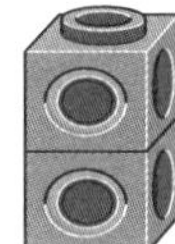 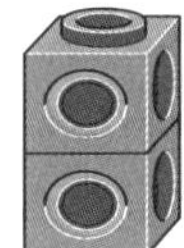  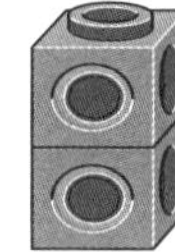 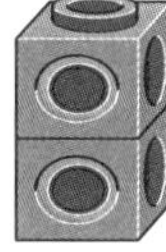 

Andy uses the cubes to make towers 3 cubes high.

How many towers can he make?

Andy can make [ ] towers.

Reflect

Explain how you would work out that 15 ÷ 3 = 5.

→ Textbook 3A p152

3 times-table

1 Which 3 times-table fact does each picture show?

a) 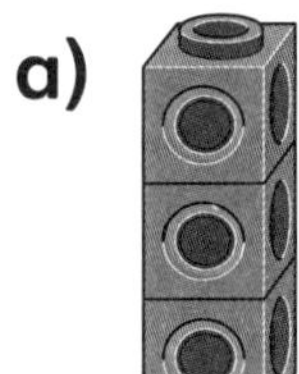 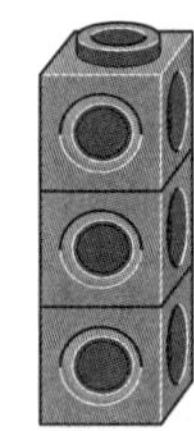 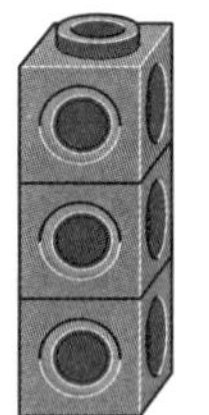 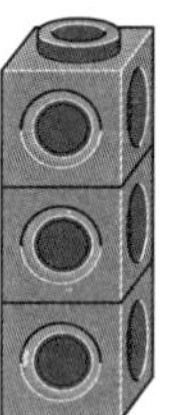 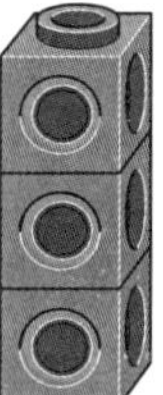

☐ × ☐ = ☐

b) 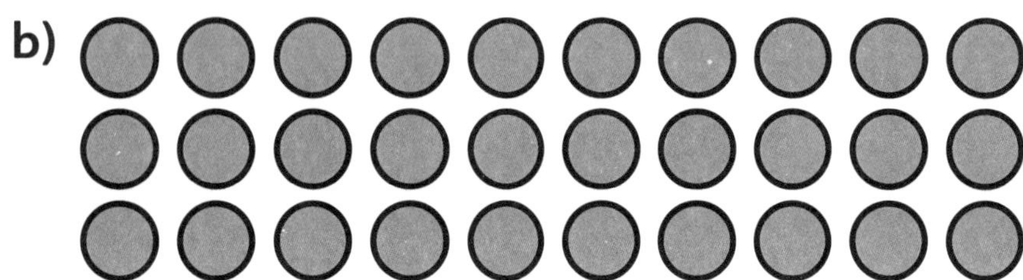

☐ × ☐ = ☐

c) 

☐ × ☐ = ☐

2 Work out the answers to these multiplications.

a) 0 × 3 = ☐

b) 9 × 3 = ☐

c) ☐ = 7 × 3

d) ☐ × 3 = 24

3 Join the calculations to the correct circle. Complete any calculations that are already joined to a circle.

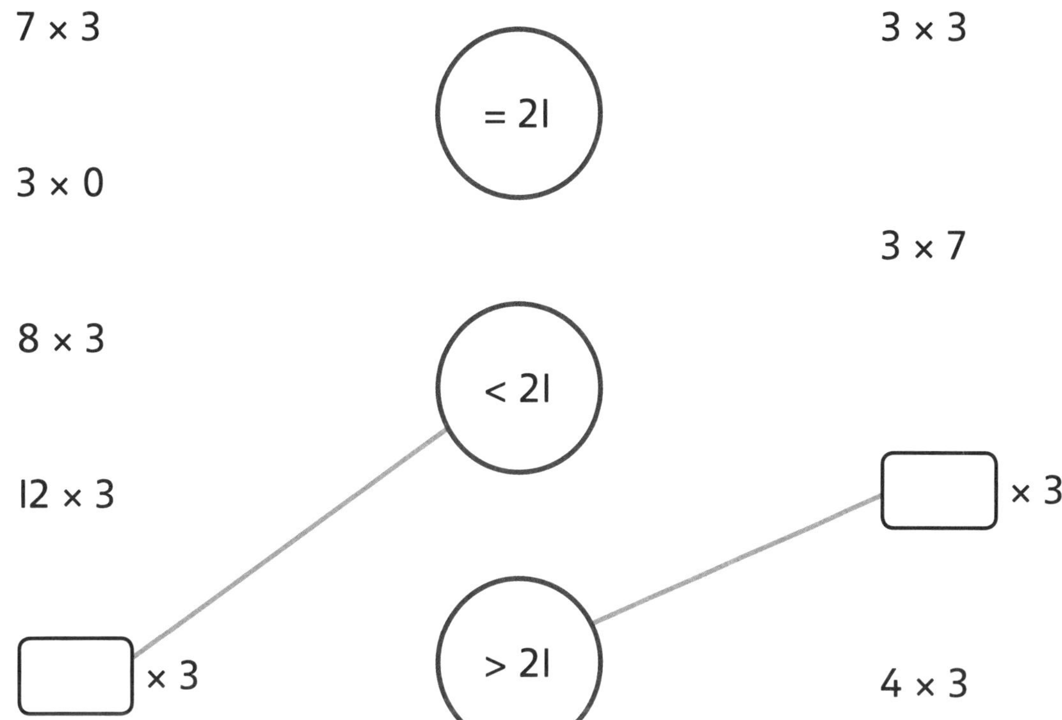

4 Work out the answers to these divisions.

a) 36 ÷ 3 = □

b) 18 ÷ 3 = □

c) 21 ÷ 3 = □

d) 0 ÷ 3 = □

e) □ ÷ 3 = 4

f) □ ÷ 3 = 1

g) 15 ÷ □ = 5

5 Complete using <, > or =

a) 5 × 3 ◯ 8

b) 3 × 7 ◯ 20

c) 3 × 3 ◯ 3 + 3 + 3 + 3

d) 5 × 3 ◯ 3 × 5

e) 8 + 8 + 8 ◯ 3 × 7

f) 4 × 3 ◯ 3 × 6

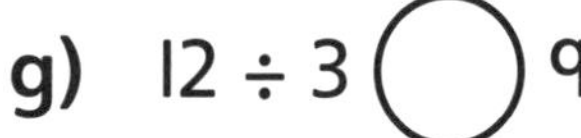

g) 12 ÷ 3 ◯ 9

h) 33 ÷ 3 ◯ 10

i) 15 ÷ 3 ◯ 18 ÷ 3

j) 9 × 3 ◯ 9 ÷ 3

I wonder if you always have to work out the calculations.

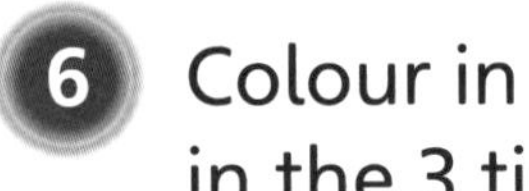

6 Colour in all the numbers in the 3 times-table.

What patterns do you notice? Explain them to your friend.

1	2	3	4	5	6	7	8	9	10
11	12	13	14	15	16	17	18	19	20
21	22	23	24	25	26	27	28	29	30
31	32	33	34	35	36	37	38	39	40
41	42	43	44	45	46	47	48	49	50
51	52	53	54	55	56	57	58	59	60
61	62	63	64	65	66	67	68	69	70
71	72	73	74	75	76	77	78	79	80
81	82	83	84	85	86	87	88	89	90
91	92	93	94	95	96	97	98	99	100

Reflect

Roll two dice. Add the two numbers together and multiply your answer by 3.

See how many times you can do this in 1 minute. Go!

→ Textbook 3A p156

Multiplying by 4

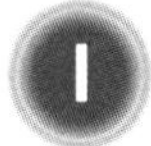

a) How many muffins are there?

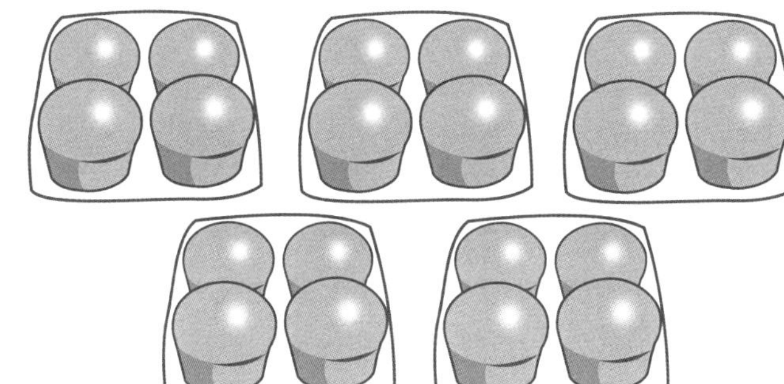

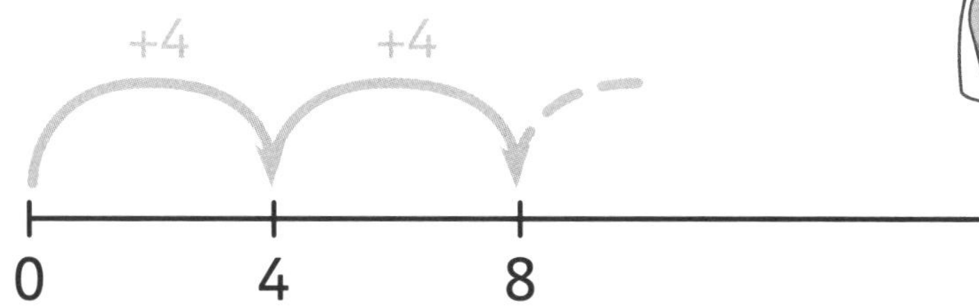

□ × □ = □

There are □ muffins.

b) How many glasses are there?

□ × □ = □

There are □ glasses.

2 Max is drawing squares and counting the sides.

Complete the table.

Number of squares	0	1	2	5	8	11	12
Number of sides			8				

3 A plank is 4 metres long.

What is the total length of the planks?

☐ × ☐ = ☐

4 The prices of a mug and a teddy bear are shown.

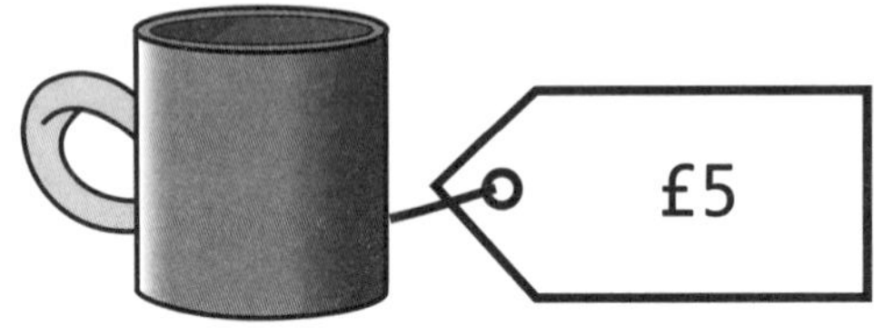

a) Aki buys 7 teddy bears.

What is the total cost?

☐ ○ ☐ = ☐

The total cost is £☐.

b) Aki also buys 4 mugs.

What is the total cost of the mugs?

The total cost is £☐.

c) How much did Aki spend in total?

☐ ○ ☐ = ☐

In total, Aki spent £☐.

5 Use Olivia's rule to multiply these numbers by 4.

a) 21 ____________________

b) 50 ____________________

c) 27 ____________________

CHALLENGE

6 There are 4 trading cards in a pack.

Ali buys 7 packs.

Mark buys 5 packs.

How many cards do they have altogether?

____

____

Altogether they have [ ] cards.

Reflect

How do you multiply a number by 4?

- ____
- ____
- ____
-

→ Textbook 3A p160

Dividing by 4

1 **a)** Jelly beans are shared equally between 4 children.

How many beans does each child get?

☐ ÷ ☐ = ☐

Each child gets ☐ jelly beans.

b) Apples are packed into boxes of 4.

How many boxes of apples can be made?

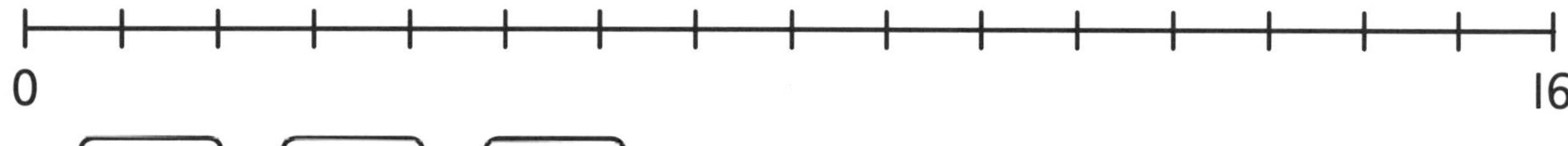

☐ ÷ ☐ = ☐

☐ boxes of apples can be made.

2 Liam counts 20 cat legs.

How many cats are there?

☐ ÷ ☐ = ☐

There are ☐ cats.

3 Use the array to work out 32 ÷ 4.

32 ÷ 4 = ☐

4 28 biscuits are shared equally between 4 plates.

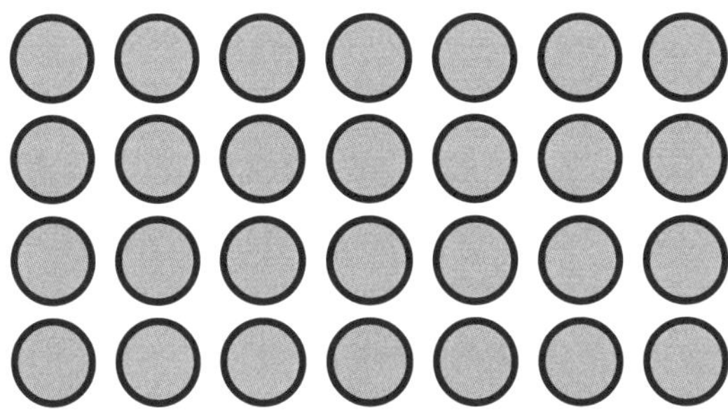
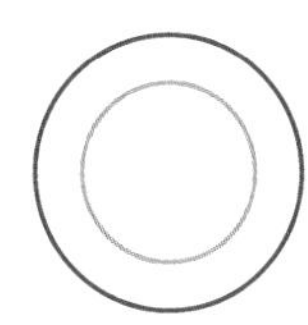
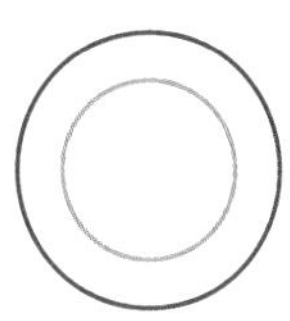
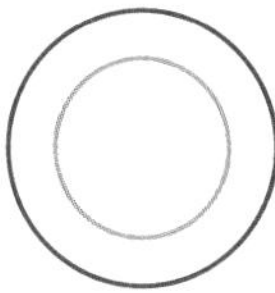
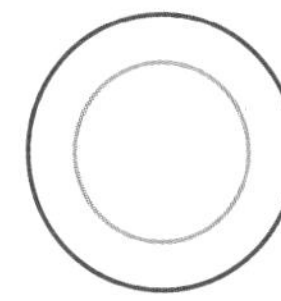

How many biscuits are there on each plate?

There are ☐ biscuits on each plate.

5 A magazine costs £4.

How many magazines can Richard buy with this note?

Richard can buy ☐ magazines.

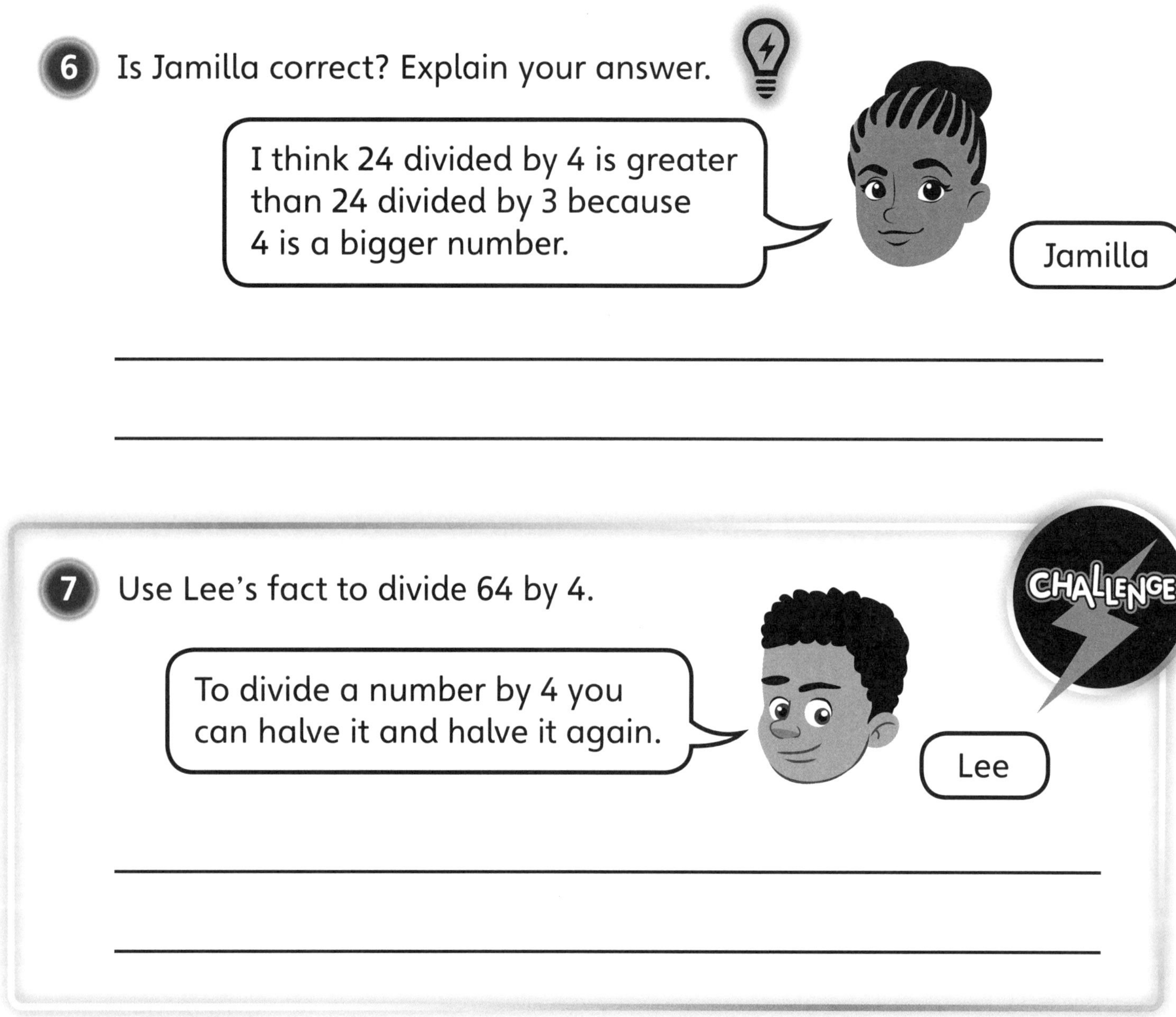

Reflect

Draw a picture to explain why, when you divide by 4, it is the same as dividing by 2 and dividing by 2 again.

→ Textbook 3A p164

4 times-table

1 Which fact from the 4 times-table does each picture show?

a) 

b)

c)

☐ × ☐ = ☐

2 Complete the multiplications.

a) 5 × 4 = ☐

b) ☐ = 1 × 4

c) 4 × 9 = ☐

d) 4 × 3 = ☐

e) ☐ × 4 = 28

f) ☐ × 4 = 44

g) 0 = ☐ × 4

h) 48 = 12 × ☐

3 **a)** Circle the numbers that are in the 4 times-table.

16 20 48 11 28 0 52 40 400

b) Explain how Andy knows this so quickly.

c) Is Zac correct?

Convince your friend.

4 Complete the missing numbers to make the calculations correct.

a) 36 ÷ 4 = ☐

b) 28 ÷ 4 = ☐

c) 40 ÷ 4 = ☐

d) 8 ÷ 4 = ☐

e) ☐ = 20 ÷ 4

f) ☐ = 32 ÷ 4

g) ☐ ÷ 4 = 3

h) ☐ ÷ 4 = 11

5 Complete using <, > or =

a) 2 × 4 ◯ 6

b) 4 + 4 + 8 ◯ 4 × 4

c) 9 × 4 ◯ 10 × 4

d) 8 × 3 ◯ 6 × 4

e) 20 ÷ 4 ◯ 16

f) 40 ÷ 4 ◯ 10

g) 12 ÷ 4 ◯ 24 ÷ 4

h) 8 ÷ 4 ◯ 6 ÷ 3

Remember, you can do most of these without having to work them out.

6 Work out the missing numbers.

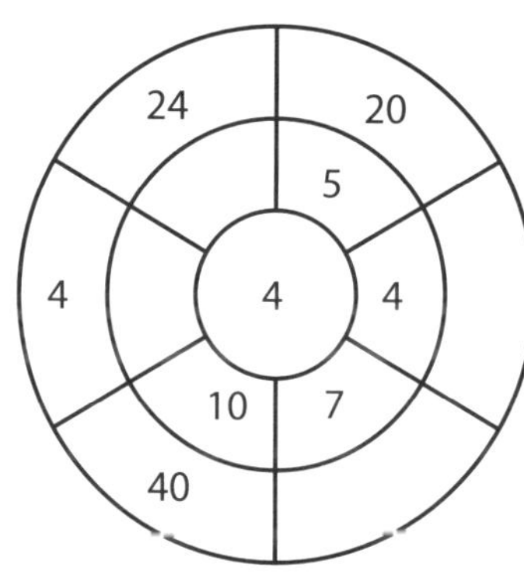

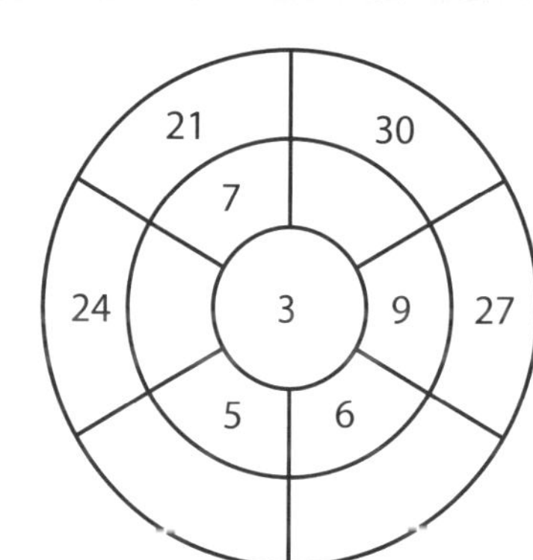

Reflect

12 is in the 3 times-table and the 4 times-table.

Find some other numbers that are in the 3 and the 4 times-table.

- ______________________
- ______________________
-

Is there a pattern?

→ Textbook 3A p168

Multiplying by 8

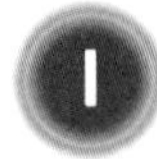

1 a) How many pens are there altogether?

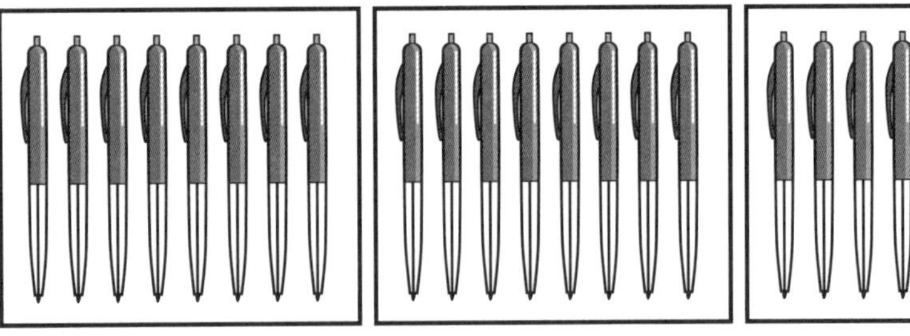

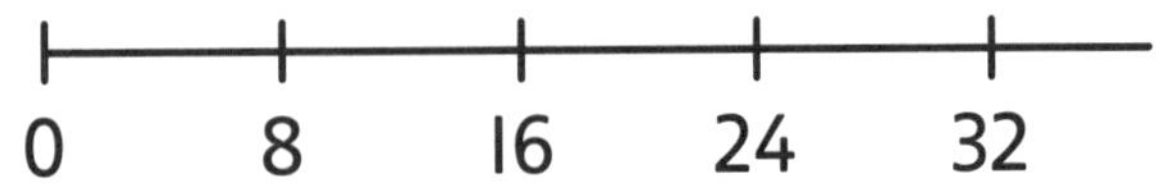

☐ × ☐ = ☐

There are ☐ pens.

b) How many flowers are there?

☐ × ☐ = ☐

There are ☐ flowers.

2 A spider has 8 legs.

How many legs do 5 spiders have?

☐ × ☐ = ☐

5 spiders have ☐ legs.

3 What is the mass of the dog?

☐ × ☐ = ☐

The mass of the dog is ☐ kg.

4 There are some biscuits in 4 jars.

How many biscuits are there in total?

☐ × ☐ = ☐

There are ☐ biscuits in total.

5 a) Lexi multiplied her number by 4 and got 28.

What is Lexi's number multiplied by 8?

Lexi's number multiplied by 8 is ☐.

b) If ☆ × 8 = 64, what is ☆ × 4?

☆ × 4 = ☐

6 Here is a rule for multiplying by 8.

To multiply 12 by 8
First, double 12, which is 24.
Next, double 24, which is 48.
Then double 48, which is 96.
So, 12 × 8 = 96.

Use this rule to work out:

a) 20 multiplied by 8.

20 × 8 = ☐

b) 37 multiplied by 8.

37 × 8 = ☐

I am going to add to help me work out what double 37 is.

Reflect

If you know that 6 × 4 = 24, how can you work out 6 × 8?

Explain your answer.

→ Textbook 3A p172

Dividing by 8

a) Pegs are packed into packs of 8.

There are 24 pegs.

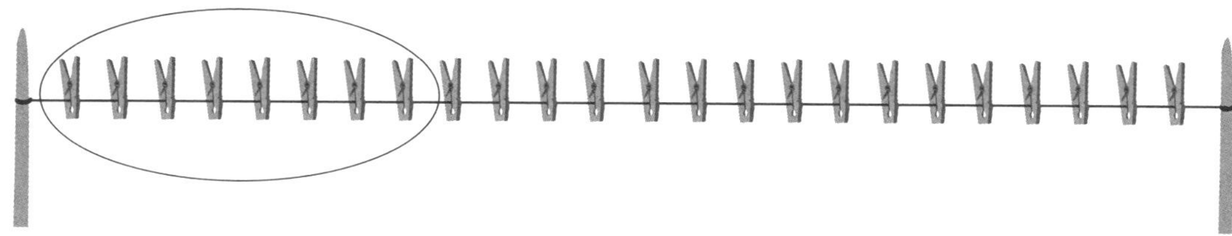

How many packs can you make?

☐ ÷ ☐ = ☐

You can make ☐ packs of pegs.

b) A lorry has 8 wheels.

How many lorries are there?

☐ ÷ ☐ = ☐

There are ☐ lorries.

2 8 balls are shared equally between 8 cats.

How many balls does each cat get?

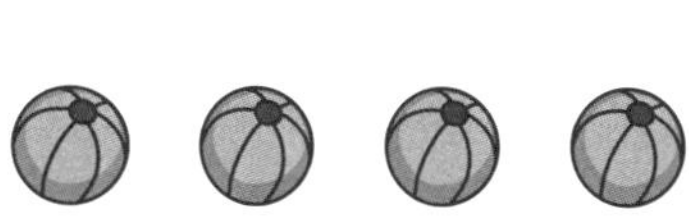

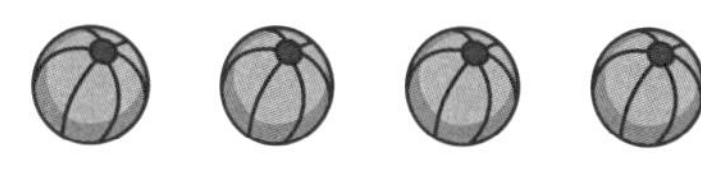

☐ ÷ ☐ = ☐

Each cat gets ☐ ball/balls.

3 Millie is holding some octagons.

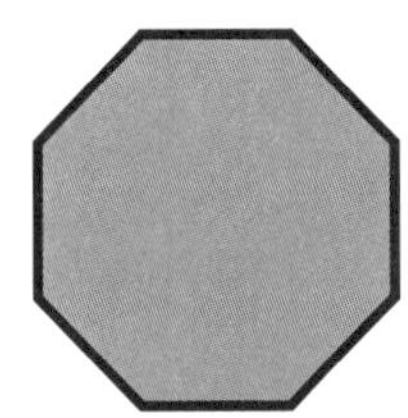

An octagon has 8 sides. There are 48 sides in total.

How many octagons does she have?

☐ ÷ ☐ = ☐

Millie has ☐ octagons.

4 Use the diagrams to help you work out the divisions.

a)

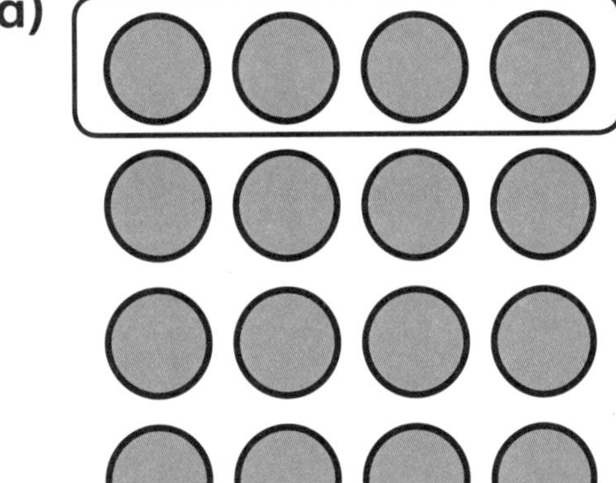

$16 \div 4 =$ ☐

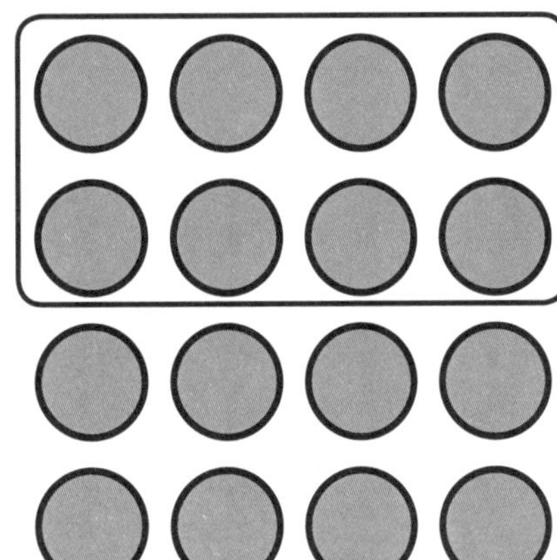

$16 \div 8 =$ ☐

b)

$40 \div 4 =$ ☐

$40 \div 8 =$ ☐

5 A bag of counters is shared equally between 8 children.

Each child receives 4 counters.

How many counters were in the bag?

☐ ◯ ☐ = ☐

☐ counters were in the bag.

6 CHALLENGE

When I divide my number by 4, I get 6.

Jamie

Jamie divides her number by 8.

What answer does she get?

Show your working.

____

____

____

Reflect

Write or draw the steps to work out 16 divided by 8.

-
-
-
-
-

→ Textbook 3A p176

8 times-table

1 Which 8 times-table fact does each picture show?

a) 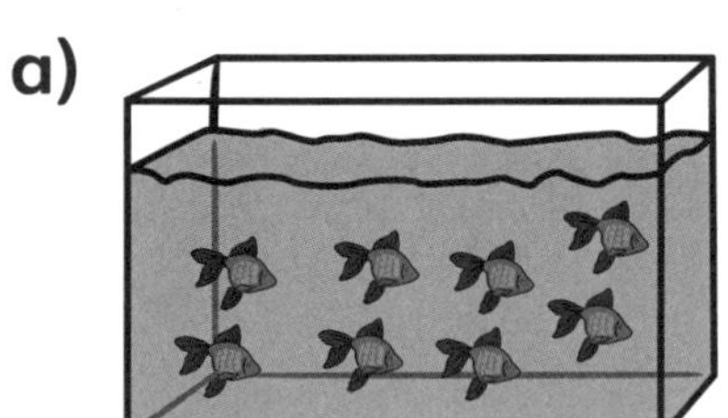 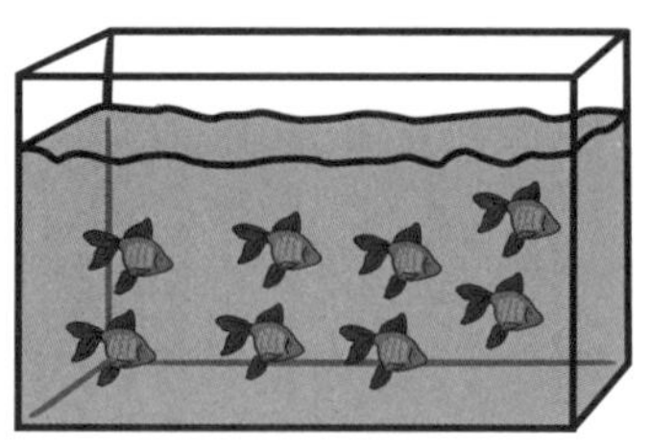

☐ × 8 = ☐ fish

b) 

☐ × ☐ = ☐ spots

c) 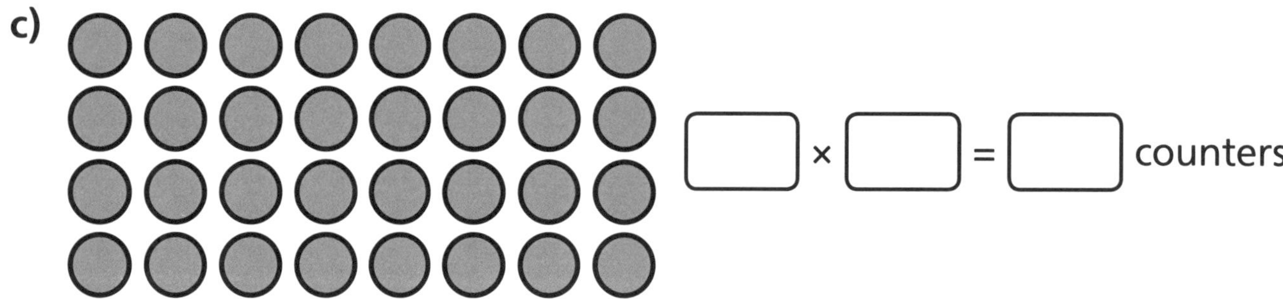

☐ × ☐ = ☐ counters

2 Work out the answers.

a) 6 × 8 = ☐

b) 0 × 8 = ☐

c) ☐ = 12 × 8

d) 5 × 8 = ☐

e) ☐ = 8 × 10

f) 64 = 8 × ☐

g) ☐ × 8 = 8

h) ☐ × 8 = 56

3 Fill in the missing numbers.

a)
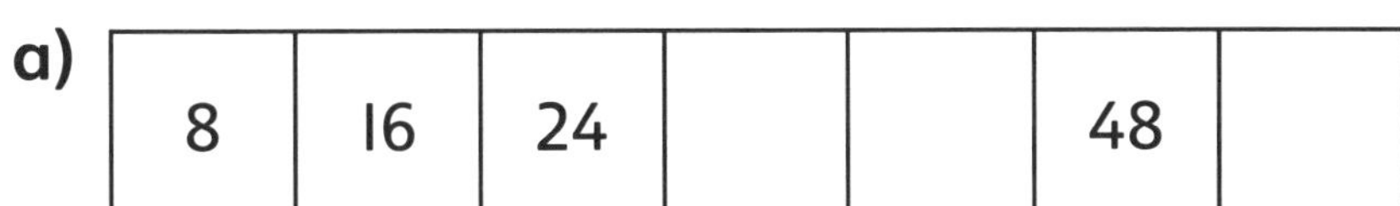

8	16	24			48	

b)

96	88		72			48	

c)

40					80

d)

40					0

4 Work out the missing numbers.

a) $40 \div 8 = \square$

b) $\square = 24 \div 8$

c) $32 \div 8 = \square$

d) $\square = 96 \div 8$

e) $\square = 72 \div 8$

f) $\square \div 8 = 10$

g) $\square \div 8 = 1$

h) $\square \div 8 = 0$

5 Complete the sentences using <, > or =

a) $2 \times 8 \bigcirc 10$

b) $5 \times 8 \bigcirc 6 \times 8$

c) $4 \times 8 \bigcirc 8 \times 4$

d) $8 \times 3 \bigcirc 10 \times 8$

e) $32 \div 8 \bigcirc 4$

f) $40 \div 8 \bigcirc 20$

g) $16 \div 8 \bigcirc 8 \div 4$

h) $88 \div 8 \bigcirc 88 \div 7$

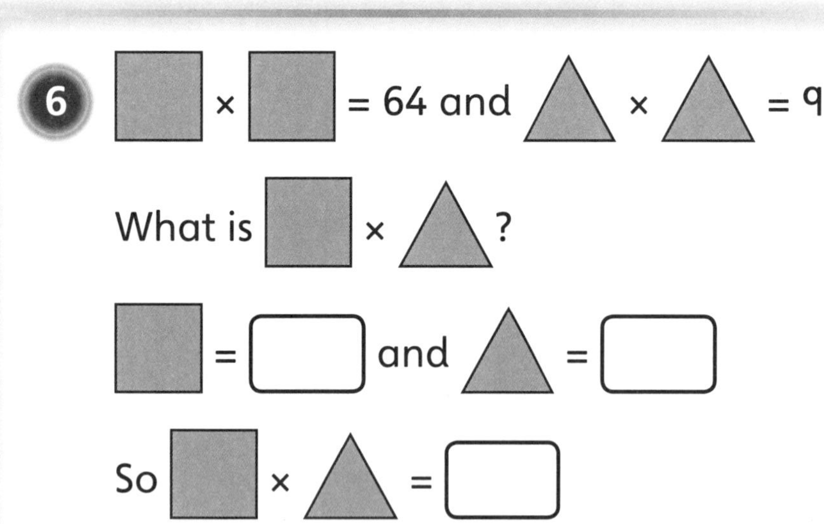

Reflect

How many times-table facts can you write in this table?

Some have been done for you.

The answer is 0	The answer is greater than 30, but less than 40	The answer is 40	The answer is greater than 70
0 × 3 = 0	4 × 8 = 32	2 × 20 = 40	10 × 9 = 90

What do you notice about the numbers in the facts in the first column?

→ Textbook 3A p180

Problem solving – multiplication and division 1

1 a) What is the total score?

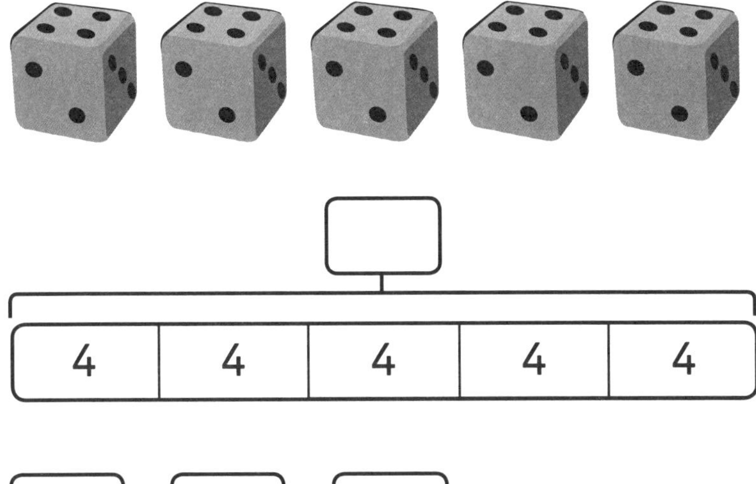

☐ × ☐ = ☐

The total score is ☐ .

b) How many rulers are there?

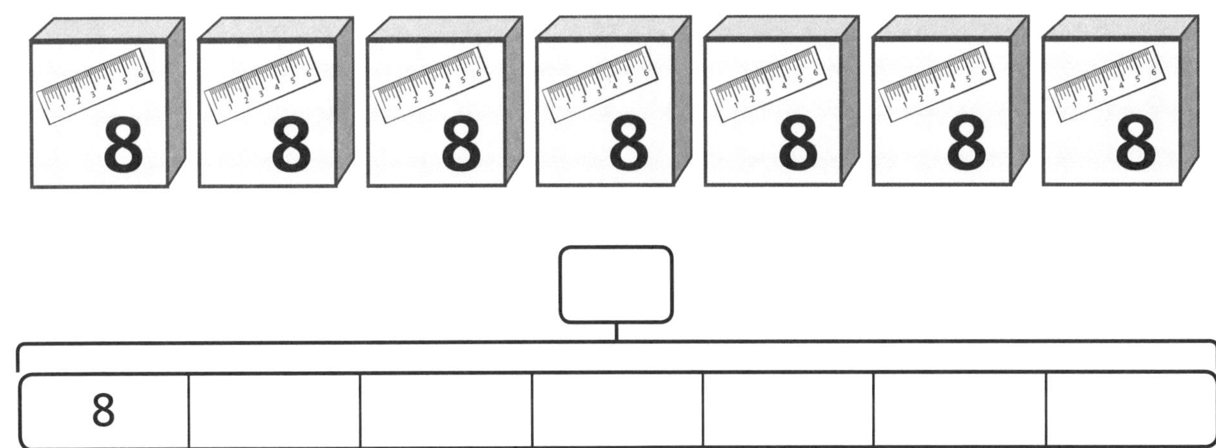

☐ ◯ ☐ = ☐

There are ☐ rulers.

2 There is an equal number of arrows on four paths.

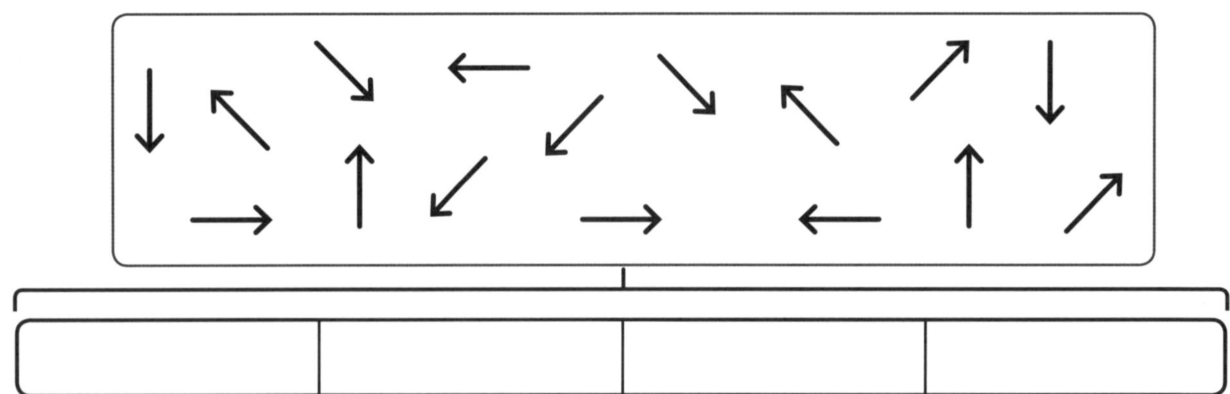

How many arrows are on each path?

☐ ÷ ☐ = ☐

Each path has ☐ arrows.

3 These buttons are put into bags of 8.

How many bags are needed?

☐ bags are needed.

4 A game costs £3.

Marcus buys 5 games.

How much do 5 games cost in total?

Draw a bar model.

Write down the calculation.

☐ ○ ☐ = ☐

5 games cost £☐.

5 How much does each box weigh?

CHALLENGE

8 kg
8 kg 8 kg
8 kg 8 kg 8 kg

Each box weighs ☐ kg.

Reflect

Aki is solving a multiplication word problem. The answer is 24.

What could the question be?

→ Textbook 3A p184

Problem solving – multiplication and division 2

1 **a)** How many jam tarts are on each tray?

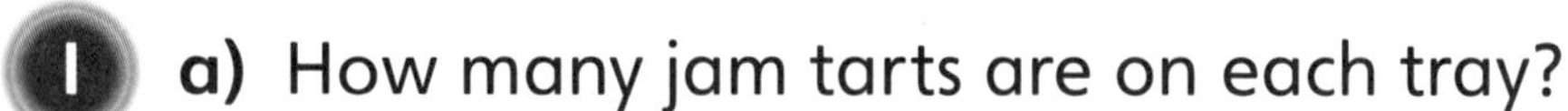

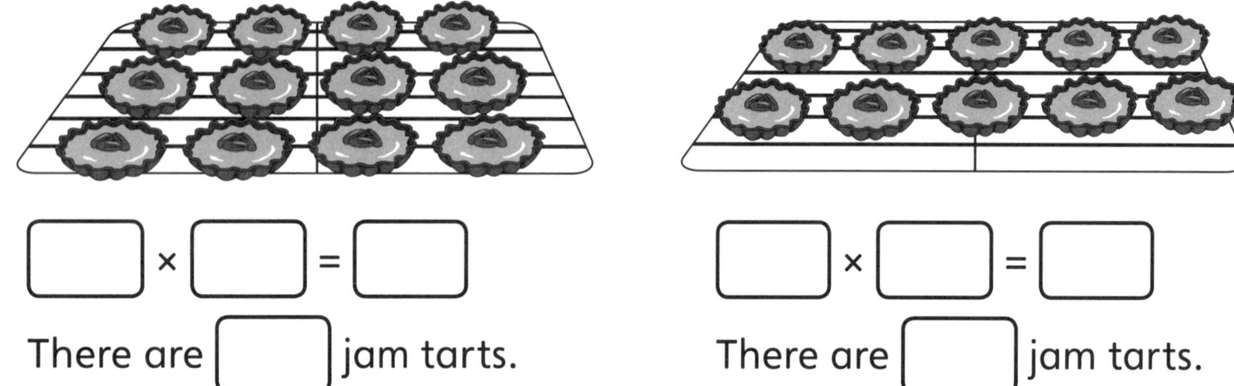

☐ × ☐ = ☐

There are ☐ jam tarts.

☐ × ☐ = ☐

There are ☐ jam tarts.

b) How many jam tarts are there in total?

☐ + ☐ = ☐

There are ☐ jam tarts in total.

2 How many counters are there in total?

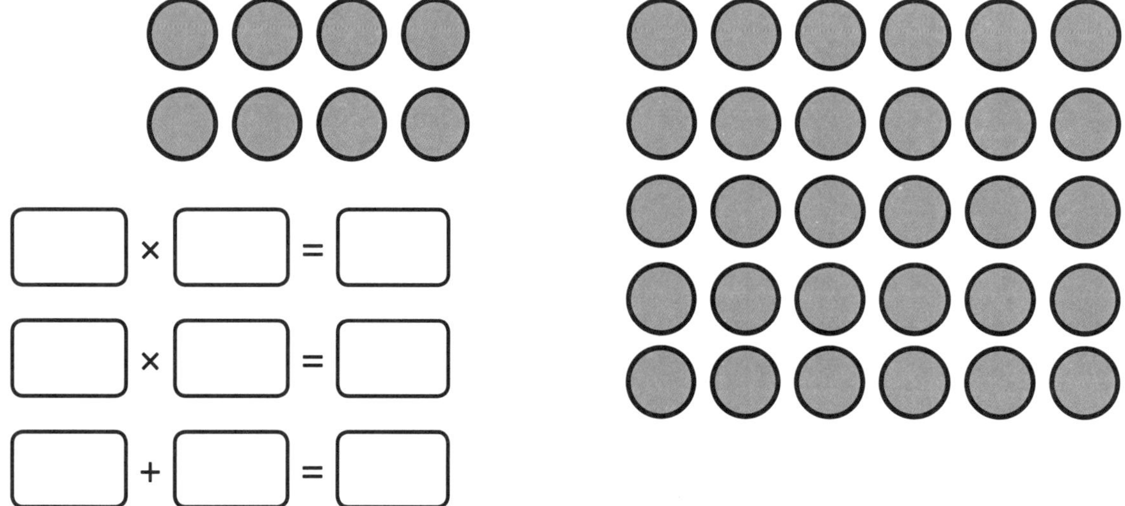

☐ × ☐ = ☐

☐ × ☐ = ☐

☐ + ☐ = ☐

There are ☐ counters in total.

3 Robots are packed in boxes of 8.

Amira

Jamie

a) Who has more robots?

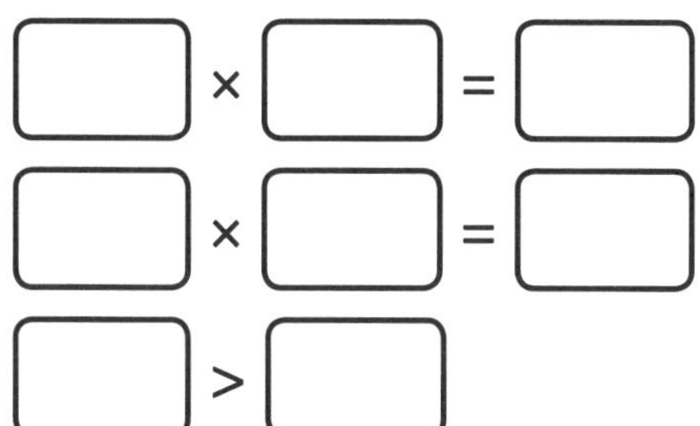

_______________ has more robots.

b) How many more robots do they have?

They have ☐ more robots.

4 **a)** How much do 7 buckets cost altogether?

7 buckets cost £☐.

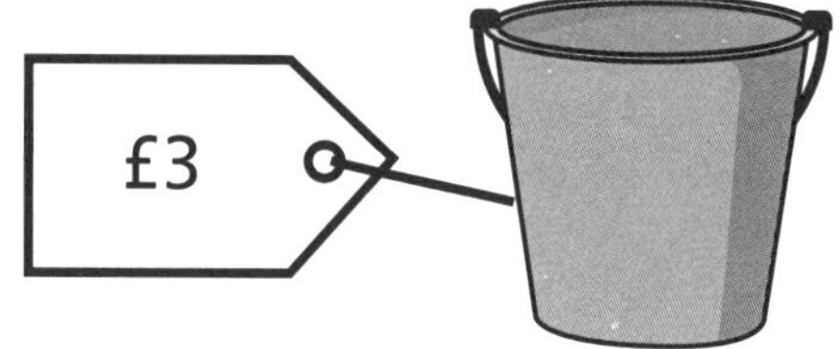

b) How many beach balls can you buy with £40?

You can buy ☐ beach balls.

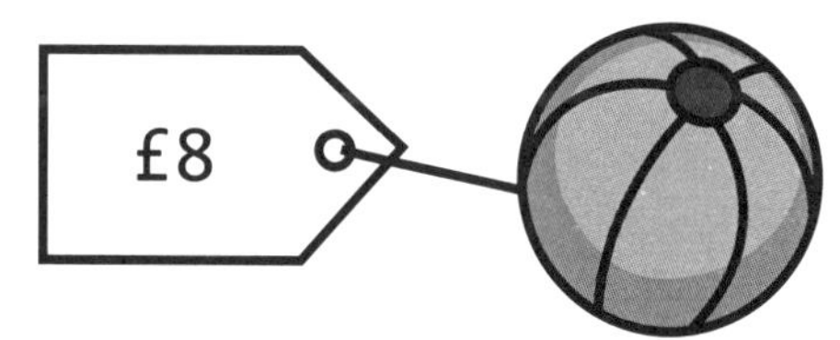

CHALLENGE

5 Cards come in boxes of 10.

The cards from 6 boxes are put into piles.

There are 4 cards in each pile.

How many piles of 4 cards can be made?

☐ piles of 4 cards can be made.

Reflect

Make up a multiplication or division question about this price list.

Challenge your friend to answer it.

____

____

____

→ Textbook 3A p188

Understanding divisibility 1

1 Lexi has 11 lollipop sticks.

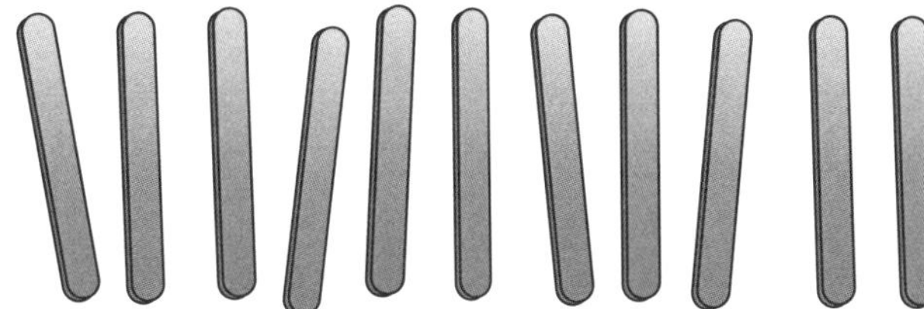

She makes squares, like this.

a) Draw the squares that Lexi makes.

b) How many complete squares can Lexi make?

Lexi can make ☐ complete squares.

c) What is the remainder?

The remainder is ☐ lollipop sticks.

d) What if Lexi makes triangles with the sticks?

How many complete triangles can she make?

What is the remainder?

There are ☐ complete triangles and the remainder is ☐.

Now Lexi is using lollipop sticks to make pentagons.

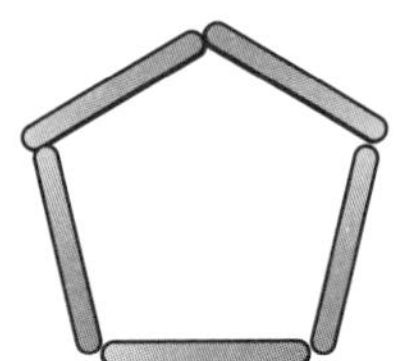

a) Complete the table.

Lollipop sticks	Working	Number of pentagons	Remainder
12		2	2
13		2	
14			
15			
16			
		4	3

b) What is the greatest number of lollipop sticks that can be left over?

Explain why.

CHALLENGE

3 Max makes square blocks from cubes, like this.

He makes 5 square blocks and has a remainder of 3 cubes.

How many cubes did Max start with?

Max started with ☐ cubes.

Reflect

Explain why Aki is correct.

When you divide by 5, the greatest remainder is 4.

Aki

→ Textbook 3A p192

Understanding divisibility 2

1 Share 13 cakes between 2 plates.

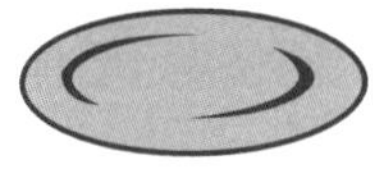 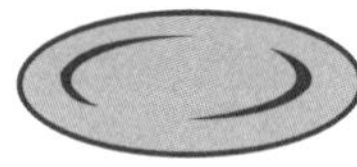

How many cakes are on each plate?

How many are left over?

There are ☐ cakes on each plate and ☐ cake left over.

13 ÷ 2 = ☐ remainder ☐

2 The cakes are packed into boxes of 3.

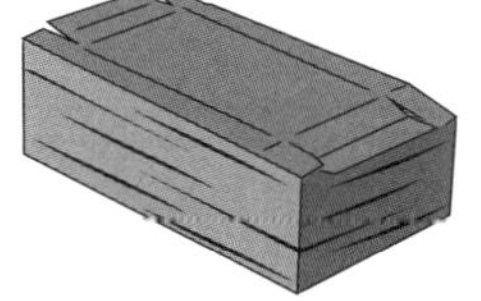

How many complete boxes can be made?

How many cakes are left over?

There are ☐ complete boxes and ☐ cake left over.

13 ÷ 3 = ☐ remainder ☐

3 These coins are shared among 5 people.

How many coins does each person get?

How many coins are left over?

☐ ÷ ☐ = ☐ remainder ☐

4 Use counters to work out:

a) 15 ÷ 2 = ☐ remainder ☐

b) 15 ÷ 3 = ☐ remainder ☐

c) 15 ÷ 4 = ☐ remainder ☐

d) 15 ÷ 5 = ☐ remainder ☐

e) 15 ÷ 6 = ☐ remainder ☐

5 **a)** Look at these calculations.

Circle the three that will have a remainder.

How do you know?

13 ÷ 3	20 ÷ 5	19 ÷ 4	28 ÷ 10	30 ÷ 2	48 ÷ 8

b) Work out the answers to the calculations that will have a remainder.

☐ ÷ ☐ = ☐ remainder ☐

☐ ÷ ☐ = ☐ remainder ☐

☐ ÷ ☐ = ☐ remainder ☐

6 **a)** When I divide a number by 4, the remainder is 1. 

What could the number be?

Find three possible numbers.

____

____

b) When Jamie divides her number by 5, the remainder is 7.

How do you know Jamie is not correct?

____

____

7 Work out the missing number.

☐ ÷ 5 = 4 remainder 4

Reflect

What is the remainder when each of these numbers is divided by 3?

3, 6, 9, 12, 15, 18, 21, 24, 27, 30

How do you know?

What numbers will give a remainder 1 when you divide by 3?

____

____

____

→ Textbook 3A p196

Related facts – multiplication and division

1 18 bean bags are arranged in an array.

There are 3 rows.

There are 6 columns.

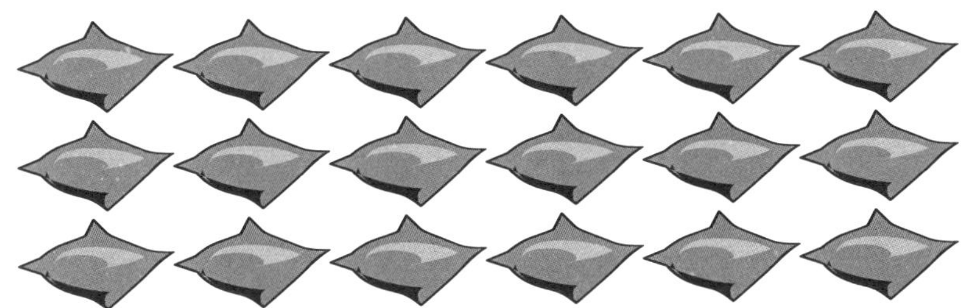

Complete two multiplication facts and two division facts for this array.

☐ × ☐ = ☐ ☐ ÷ ☐ = ☐

☐ × ☐ = ☐ ☐ ÷ ☐ = ☐

2 What multiplication and division facts can you see?

a)

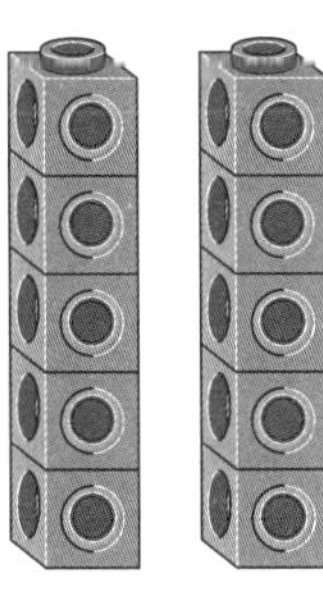

b)

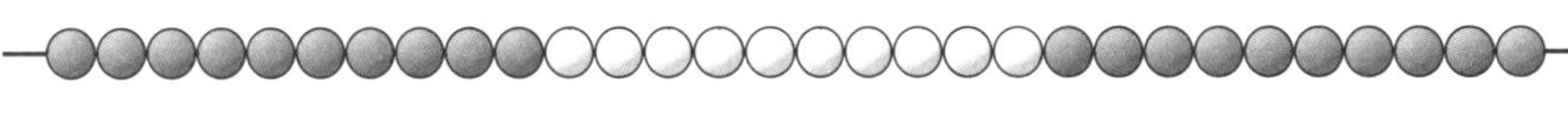

☐ × ☐ = ☐

☐ ÷ ☐ = ☐

☐ ÷ ☐ = ☐

☐ × ☐ = ☐

☐ ÷ ☐ = ☐

3 Find eight multiplication and division facts for this array.

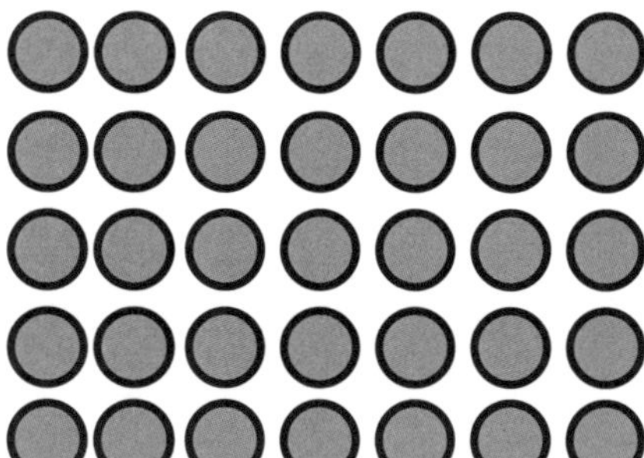

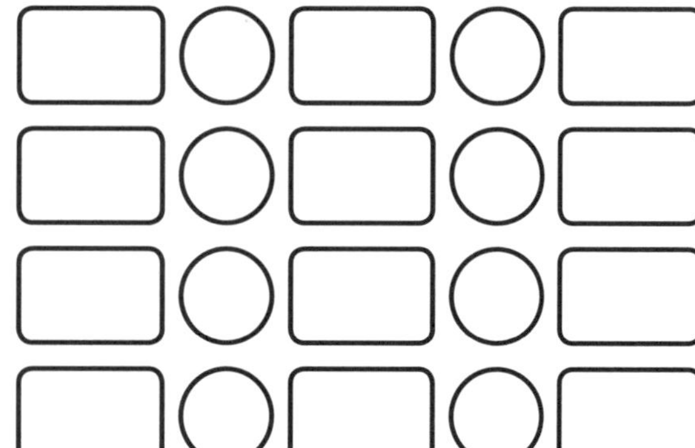

4 Match each calculation to the answer it works out.

6 × 10 = 60	number of leaflets in each pack
60 ÷ 10 = 6	number of packs
60 ÷ 6 = 10	total number of leaflets
10 × 6 = 60	

5 Work out the value of each symbol. 

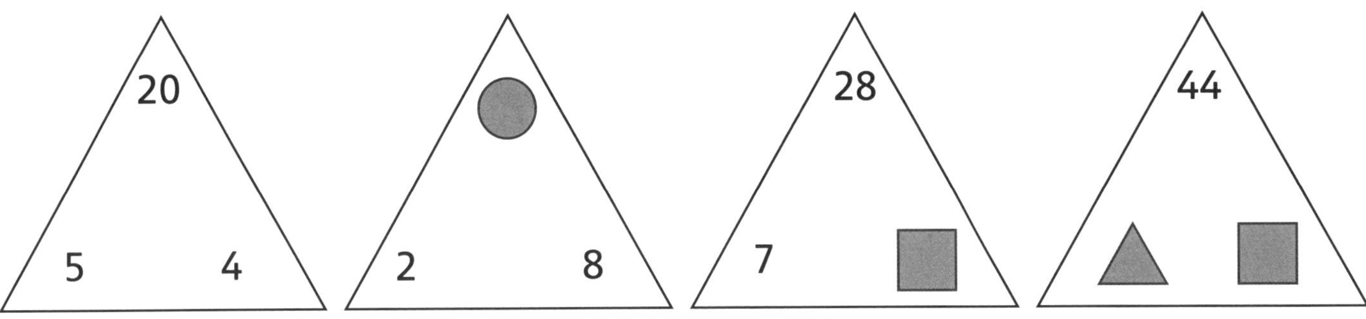

● = [ ]   ■ = [ ]   ▲ = [ ]

6 **a)** 8 × 20 = 160

Use this to work out 160 ÷ 8 = [ ]

b) 195 ÷ 5 = 39

Use this to work out 39 × 5 = [ ]

Reflect

Write down as many multiplication and division facts as you can for this array.

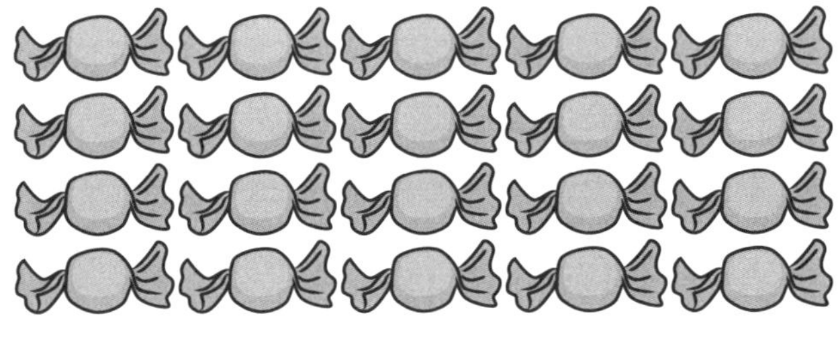

- ______________________
- ______________________
- ______________________
- ______________________
- ______________________

→ Textbook 3A p200

End of unit check

My journal

You now know the 2, 3, 4, 5, 8 and 10 times-tables.

Work out a number that could go into each box.

What strategy did you use?

	My number
a) A number in the 2 and 5 times-tables greater than 25	
b) A number in the 3, 4 and 8 times-tables	
c) A number in the 8 and 10 times-tables less than 50	
d) A number in the 3, 4 and 5 times-tables	
e) A number in the 2, 3, 4, 5, 8 and 10 times-tables	

Power check

How do you feel about your work in this unit?   

Power play

Time Trial

a) How quickly can you complete these times-table wheels?

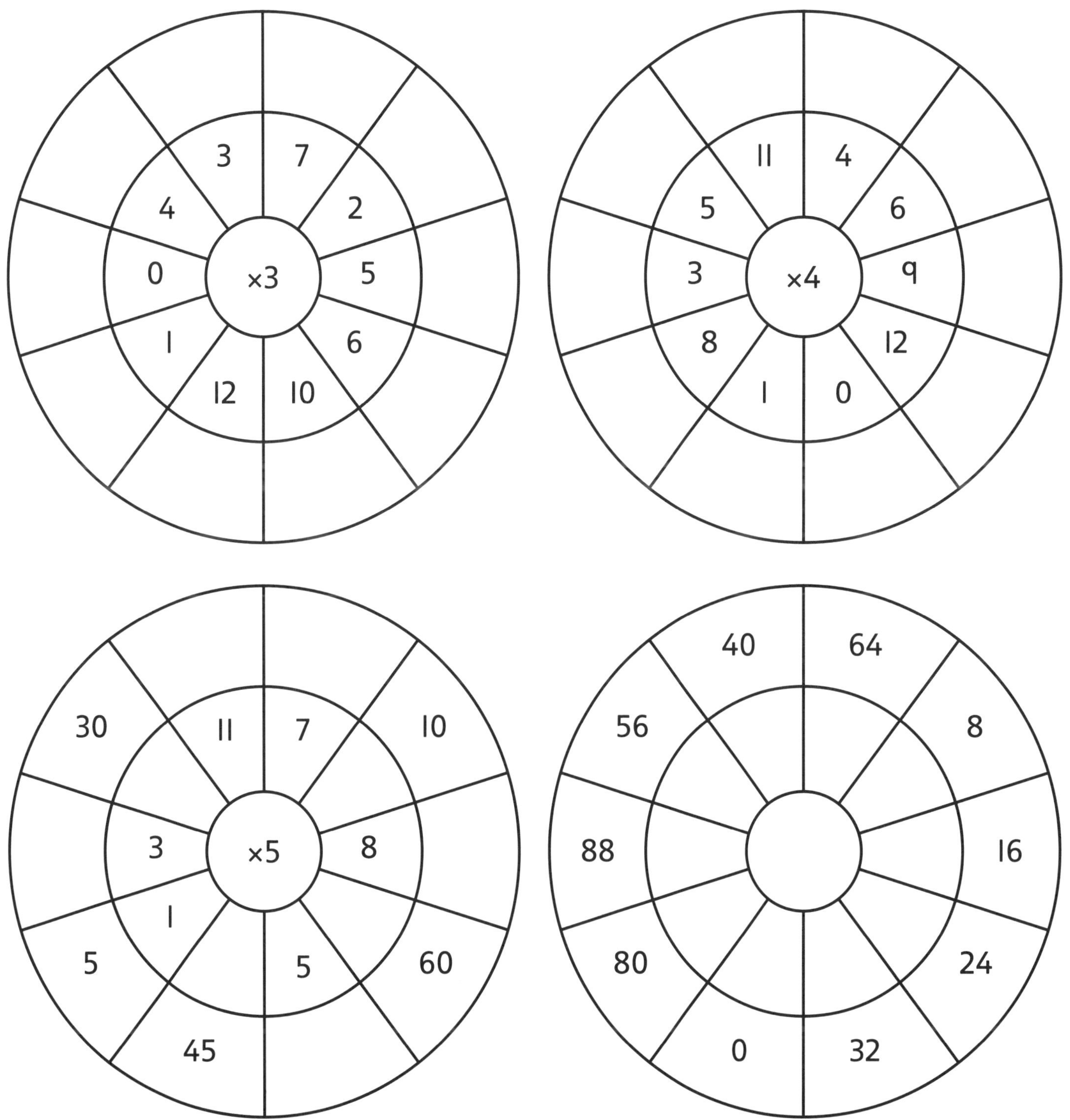

b) This is a different type of wheel. Can you find the missing numbers?

You can only use the 2, 3, 4, 5, 8 and 10 times-tables.

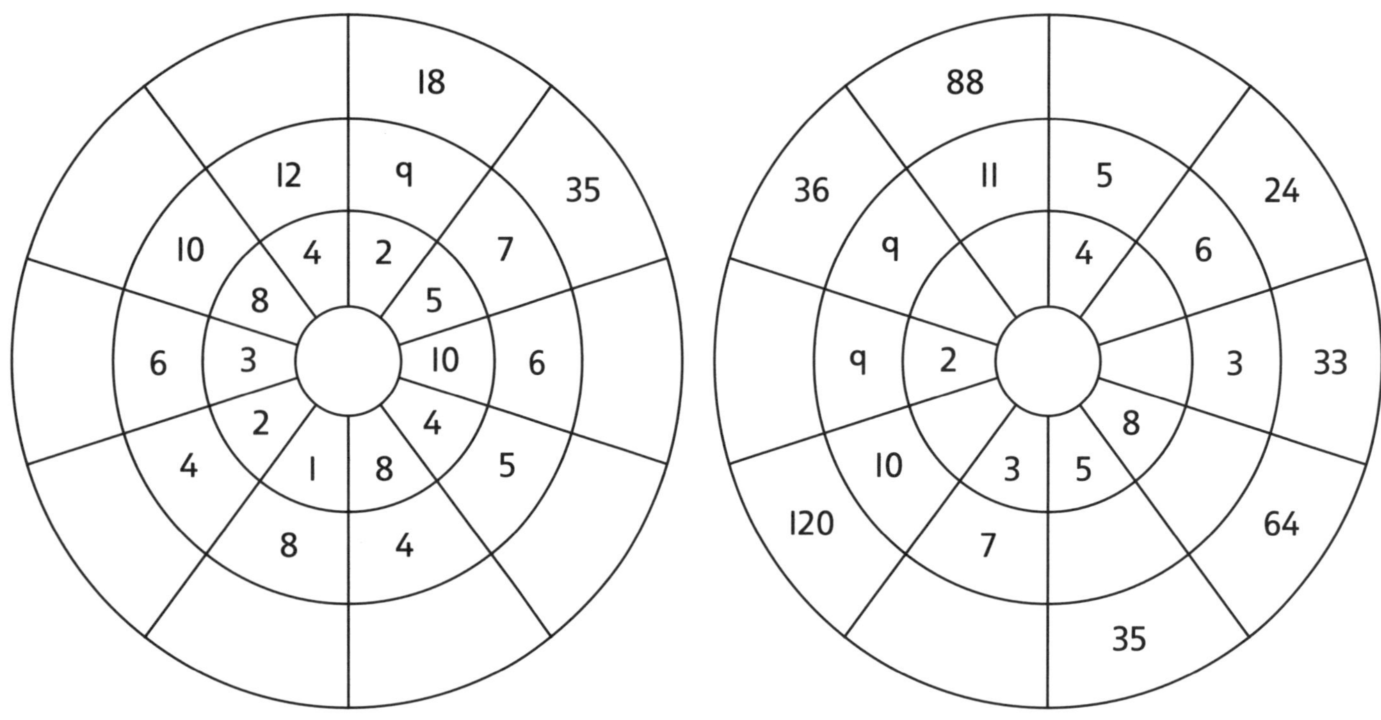

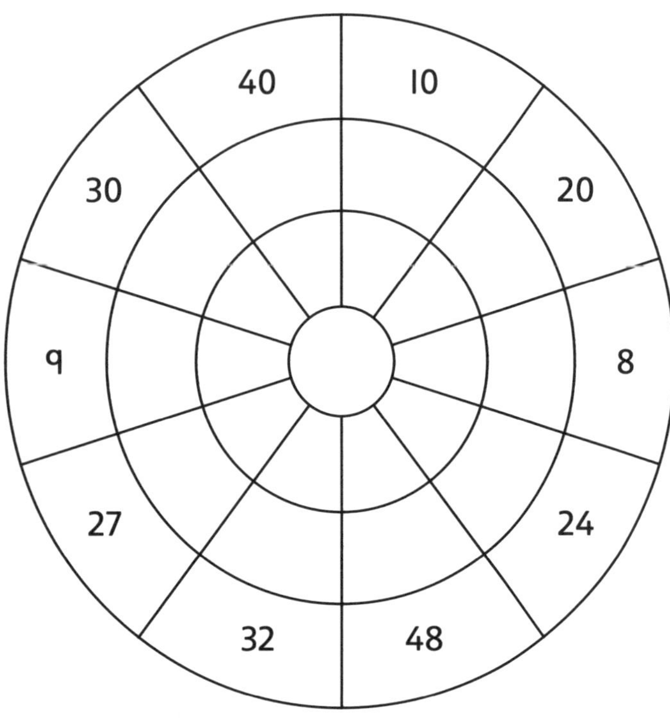

My power points

Colour in the ☆ to show what you have learnt.

Colour in the ☺ if you feel happy about what you have learnt.

Unit 1

I can ...

☆ ☺ Count in 100s

☆ ☺ Represent 1,000 using base 10 equipment and part-whole models

☆ ☺ Find 1, 10 and 100 more or less

☆ ☺ Compare and order numbers up to 1,000 using a number line

☆ ☺ Count in 50s

Unit 2

I can ...

☆ ☺ Add 1s and 10s to 3-digit numbers

☆ ☺ Subtract 1s and 10s from 3-digit numbers

☆ ☺ Add and subtract a 3-digit number and a 2-digit number

☆ ☺ Explain when to exchange 1s, 10s and 100s

☆ ☺ Add and subtract using mental and written methods

Unit 3

I can ...

- ☆ ☺ Spot addition and subtraction patterns
- ☆ ☺ Add two 3-digit numbers
- ☆ ☺ Subtract a 3-digit number from a 3-digit number
- ☆ ☺ Estimate the answer to addition and subtraction problems
- ☆ ☺ Solve problems involving addition and subtraction using a bar model

Unit 4

I can ...

- ☆ ☺ Recognise equal groups
- ☆ ☺ Multiply by 3
- ☆ ☺ Divide by 3
- ☆ ☺ Multiply by 4
- ☆ ☺ Divide by 4
- ☆ ☺ Multiply by 8
- ☆ ☺ Divide by 8
- ☆ ☺ Solve problems involving multiplication and division using a bar model
- ☆ ☺ Find a remainder when a number is divided

Keep up the good work!